Ki in Aikido

A Sampler of Ki Exercises

by
C. M. Shifflett

Round Earth Publishing
Merrifield, Virginia

Ki in Aikido:
A Sampler of Ki Exercises

By C. M. Shifflett

Round Earth Publishing
P. O. Box 3855
Merrifield, Virginia 22116

Printed in the United States of America
First Edition, Second Printing
Cover photograph by Linda Adkisson
Cover design and full-color scan by The Bluemont Company

Publisher's Cataloging in Publication
Shifflett, C. M.
    Ki in aikido : a sampler of ki exercises / by C. M. Shifflett.
    p. cm.
    Includes bibliographical references and index.
    ISBN 0-9653425-3-0   LOC 96-70236
    1. Aikido. 2. Aikido--training. 3. Ch'i (Chinese philosophy)
    I. Title.
GV1114.35.S52 1997   796.8'154

Ki in Aikido:
A Sampler of Ki Exercises

Table of Contents

Foreword _____ ix

Preface _____ xi

Acknowledgments _____ xiii

Introduction _____ *1*

What is Aikido?_____ 1

What is Ki? _____ 4
   The Concept of "Reality"_____ 6
   Images and Visualization _____ 7

What Is One-Point? _____ 8

Testing for One-Point and Ki_____ 10

Rules For Mind-Body Coordination _____ 11

What You're Really Looking For _____ 11

It's Really Just ... _____ 12
   Programming _____ 12
   Supernatural Powers _____ 13
   Faking _____ 14

Test Lists _____ 15
   Shin-Shin Toitsu Do Test List for Ki Development ___ 15
   Hitori Waza — Ki Testing for Aikido _____ 16

*The Basics*_____ *17*
   Unbendable Arm* _____ 18

Sitting_____ 21

Sitting Seiza* _____ 21
Sitting Cross-Legged* _____ 23

Rolling* _____ **24**
Rolling Backwards and Forwards* _____ 25
Rolling Backwards and Rising to a Kneel _____ 26
Back Rolls _____ 27
Forward Rolls* _____ 28
Cross-Rolls* _____ 30
Standing Rolls _____ 31
   Standing Backward Rolls _____ 31
   Standing Forward Rolls _____ 31

Standing — Hanmi _____ **32**

Tenkan* (Turning) _____ **34**

Testing Technique _____ **36**
Test One _____ 36
Test Two _____ 37
Test Three _____ 38
Magnetic Hand _____ 39
Variations _____ 40

Keep One-Point _____ *41*
The Goldfish Bowl _____ 45
Rubber Band _____ 46
Moving One-Point _____ 47
"Say One-Point" _____ 48
Rotation* _____ 49
Words _____ 50
Changing Size _____ 51
Kokyu-Dosa* _____ 52
Leaning Backward* _____ 56
Leaning Forward* _____ 57
Raising Arms* _____ 58
One-Point With Attitude _____ 59
Wrist Push* _____ 60
Freedom From Fear _____ 61
The Hum Test _____ 62

Relax Completely _____ *63*
Relaxed Mind _____ 67
Relaxation and Rigidity _____ 68
"No pain, No gain" _____ 69

Arm Swinging* _____ 70
Spinning* _____ 71
Bowing* _____ 72
The Nelsons _____ 74
"Strong" and "Soft" _____ 76
Sticky Hands _____ 77
The Linebacker Versus the Water Drop _____ 78
Stiff Fist _____ 79
What *Doesn't* He Have? _____ 80
Letting Go _____ 81

Keep Weight Underside _____ *83*
Arm Dropping* _____ 87
The Light Pole _____ 88
Dinosaurs and Sand _____ 89
Unraisable Arm* _____ 90
Unliftable Hand* _____ 91
Unliftable Body* _____ 92
Floating Below_____ 94

Extend Ki _____ *95*
Water Pump _____ 99
Unbendable Arm* _____ 100
Walking with Unbendable Arm* _____ 101
Shaking Hands _____ 102
Ki Door _____ 103
The OK Test_____ 104
Rolling With a Goal _____ 106
Block Hands_____ 107
Sankyo* _____ 108
Go with the Flow — Sankyo _____ 109
Go With the Flow — Jo Exercise_____ 110
Go With the Flow — Mini-Jo _____ 111
Go With the Flow — Arm Pulling_____ 112
Go With the Flow — Pushups _____ 113
Additive Ki _____ 114
Sending Ki _____ 115
Bouncing Ki_____ 116
Absorbtion and Extension _____ 118
Disrupting Mind — Wrist Tickle _____ 120
Mind Leading Body _____ 121
Just Do It _____ 122
Tenkan on a String _____ 123

Balloon Tenkan _____ 124
Floating-Foot Tenkan _____ 126
Rag-Doll Tenkan _____ 127
More Tenkans _____ 128
Yes and No _____ 129
Light Swords and Fire Hoses _____ 130
Ikkyo-Undo* _____ 131
Ikkyo With Attitude _____ 133
Two-Direction Exercise* _____ 134
Eight-Way Exercise* _____ 135
Attention _____ 137
Hollywood Monster _____ 138

Ki Breathing _____ **139**
Practice of Ki Breathing _____ 143
Cloud of Ki _____ 144
Rising and Falling Breath _____ 145
Expansion and Contraction _____ 146
Stopping Ki or Circling Ki _____ 147
Breathing With a Bell _____ 148

Meditation _____ **149**
Counting _____ 153
The Grid _____ 154
The Gridlock _____ 155
I Am _____ 158
Mudra of Mind-Body Unification _____ 159
The Light Bubble _____ 161
Happy or Sad _____ 162
Morihei Ueshiba Meets Rube Goldberg _____ 163
Dark Side _____ 164
Radio and TV _____ 165
Treasures _____ 167
Treasure Chest _____ 168
Point of View _____ 169
Internal Aikido Class _____ 170
Harmony and Housework _____ 171
The Spiritual Spectrum _____ 172
Right and Revenge _____ 173
Dislike and Hatred _____ 174
Give or Get _____ 175
Ahimsa _____ 176
Entoku _____ 177

Thank You _____ 178
Appreciation_____ 179
Good or Ill Will _____ 180
The Act of Blessing _____ 181
Rationale _____ 182

Books, Movies and Videos _____ *183*
Books_____ 185
Movies and Videos_____ 195

Index _____ *201*

Afterword _____ **207**

Appendix A: Ki Society Dojos
Appendix B: Additional Exercises

Foreword

Training at the Virginia Ki Society is based on the teaching of a most remarkable man, Koichi Tohei Sensei, tenth Dan in Aikido and founder of the Ki Society International. During his many years of Aikido training and teaching under Aikido's founder, Morihei Ueshiba, he rose to become the designated Chief Instructor.

During his many trips to spread the principles of Aikido he became frustrated at the rapidity with which students who seemed to "get it" during his seminars would "lose it" by his next visit. As a result he developed a series of exercises and principles of execution which were designed to "fix" the information so that it would stay longer and, when lost, be reacquired easily by the student himself or through consultation with his local instructor. Tohei Sensei formed the Ki Society to spread these principles through the world.

This year, the Virginia Ki Society celebrates the 22nd year of its founding. It seems most fitting that Carol should publish this series of observations by one student who has traveled the path and "walked the walk" of this approach to training. Having studied other martial arts before entering the seemingly mysterious world of *Ki* Development and *Ki* Aikido, her approach was uniquely hers. She questioned everything, in class and at home (and apparently even when driving her car).

In a sense you are walking with her as she brings her own, unique perspective to this study. Your perspective and reflections will be different. Consider keeping a diary of your training to share with others what you have learned while walking the path that is uniquely *yours*.

I have enjoyed reading the draft of this publication and had a few chuckles as I recalled some of Carol's questions and frustrations as she sought to make *Ki* Development a part of her being. I think you will find she has done that, and done it well. Looking for another martial art, she found a way for living. May you, the reader, do the same, wherever your path through life takes you. Carol and I hope that the information in this book may become a part of that path.

George Simcox
Virginia Ki Society
Merrifield, Virginia

Preface

This *Sampler* is intended as a brief record of exercises which we have experienced, played with, and taught to others through the years at the Virginia Ki Society Merrifield dojo and its outreach programs. They are based on the teachings of Koichi Tohei, founder of *Shin-Shin Toitsu Aikido,* as taught by George Simcox and many other teachers who have made the study of *Aikido* a challenge, a privilege and a joy.

Please note the following conventions:

☐ *Uke* is the partner who "attacks" or provides the test.

☐ *Nage* is the partner who "demonstrates" the technique or is tested.

☐ Asterisks (*) indicate exercises included in the formal *ki* test list of the Virginia Ki Society.

☐ Numbers (1, 2, 3) indicate steps in performing the exercise.

☐ Letters (a, b, c) indicate variations on a theme. The possibilities are endless.

Although *ki* exercises are in no way dangerous, improper rolling can be, and improper test technique can be uncomfortable or misleading. Please consider attending a *dojo* ("training hall") where you can receive expert training and personal attention. Appendix A is a partial listing of Ki Society *dojos* throughout the world.

This *Sampler* is not intended as a detailed treatise on *ki, ki* testing or *Aikido* nor does it necessarily present the formal teachings or opinions of the Ki Society. For more thorough information on *ki* and *Aikido,* please refer to the many excellent books and materials listed at the back of this manual, especially those by Koichi Tohei and William Reed.

And come to class.

— C. M. Shifflett

Acknowledgments

I would like to thank George Simcox, Chief Instructor of the Virginia Ki Society, Merrifield, Virginia, our Head Instructor Hal Singer, and Gregory Ford-Kohne for years (going on decades) of time, dedication and patience.

Many thanks and heartfelt gratitude to fellow travelers, helpers, and contributors including:

Linda Adkisson, Chuck Auster,

James Lee Bagby, Su Bao, Mary Kay Belter, Rev. Bill Bickford,
Gerald A. Billingsley, Sanford Blatt, David F. Bosco,
Nicholle M. Braspennickx, David C. Buchanan,

Gloria Campbell, Ying-Lai Choi, Kim-Kwok Chu,
Regina Cohen, Wendy Cohen, William A. Coti, Jim Crown,

Tom Dapogny, Linda Dattilio, Kirk Demeree, Quy V. Do,
Jon and Sharon Doner, John Dupont,
Christelle and Tiffany Dupont,

Paul Gagnon, Robert E. Gardner, Chuck Graves,
Aaron Guerrieri,

Judy Halloran, Kris Hegle, Daniel M. Henry, Julie Herbert,
Craig G. Hocker, Wayne and Andrew Hucke,

Eri Izawa, David Johnson, Patrick L. Jones, Siri Gian Khalsa,
Steve Kendall, Ed Keith, Howard Kresin, Joe Landrum,

John McLaughlin, Christine and William A. McGrath,
Richard Miller, Rebecca S. Minetto, Poupee Mol,
Rick Montminy, Evan Moore,

Aram Nersesian, Rebecca Nisley,

Michael Patruznick, Robert Pavese, Cat T. Pham,
Thien-Huong N. Pham, Minh Pham,

Will Reed, Doug Riffee, Paul Ross,

Donna D. Shirbacheh, Norma Simcox, Stephen P. Smith,
Allen Stewart, Chizuko Suzuki,

Tamara and Nora Turner, John Oldenburg, Chris Swatta,
Linda R.Shifflett,

Mark Wakefield, Steve Warner, Maxine Wright, and
Dr. Wasena F. Wright, Jr.

Introduction

What is Aikido?

Aikido is a relatively new martial art dating from the 1920's when its founder, Morihei Ueshiba (*O-Sensei*), began to develop what he eventually came to call Aikido. *Aikido* means "the way (*do*) to harmony (*ai*) with *ki*."

The Japanese ideograms (*kanji*) for *Aikido* are made up of roots and word elements which bring a wealth of concept and meaning to those who can see them for what they are.

Ai, harmony — *Ai* means to fit, to be in harmony or agreement with. The lower strokes form a square which represents a mouth or opening such as that of a teapot. The upper three strokes originally formed a lid or stopper. The combination suggests two things which harmonize or fit together, such as the lid on a teapot, the cork in a bottle, the round peg in the round hole.

Ki, spirit, breath, energy — The Japanese *ki* symbol comes from the ancient Chinese character for *Qì*, steam, made up of elements representing sun and fire, the sources of steam. The upper three strokes represent the clouds of steam rising from a boiling pot of rice with a lid and handle. The cross within the pot represents a stalk of rice with four individual grains. Together these elements compose a symbol which now indicates vapor, breath, or spirit.

Dô, way, path — The elements of the symbol represent hair on a human head and legs walking along a path or what, to my eye, appear to be the square paving sections of a sidewalk or street. The combination represents a person walking down a road. *Dô* now means a road or path in the literal sense; by extension it can mean a course of study, a weekly recreation, or a way of life.

Aikido incorporates techniques from many traditional martial arts such as *kendo*, *ju-jitsu*, and *karate*, and is rooted in the ancient Japanese *samurai* warrior tradition of *budo*.

Budo is often interpreted as the "way of the sword." However, as Will Reed (1986) points out, the symbol is made up of two parts, one representing a spear and the other meaning "to stop, or cease using" — hence *the way to stop using the sword*. It is the way, notes Saotome (1993) "to halt the danger of the thrusting blade" but not in the usual sense. *"Bu"* said Ueshiba, "is Love."

Morihei Ueshiba was an intensely religious man who was also a renowned martial artist. His transformation and integration of these two apparently separate and disparate paths began in 1925 with the challenge of a duel from a high-ranking swordsman. Ueshiba had no desire to duel, and refusing to draw his sword, he evaded his opponent's furious cuts and thrusts until the man gave up, exhausted, and begged his forgiveness.

On returning home, Ueshiba was struck by a startling vision.

All at once I understood the nature of creation: the Way of a Warrior is to manifest Divine Love, a spirit that embraces and nurtures all things. Tears of gratitude and joy streamed down my cheeks. I saw the entire earth as my home, and the sun, moon, and stars as my intimate friends. All attachment to material things vanished.

Then in 1940,

Around two o'clock in the morning as I was performing ritual purification, I suddenly forgot every martial art technique I had ever learned. All of the techniques handed down from my teachers appeared completely anew. Now they were vehicles for the cultivation of life, knowledge, virtue, and good sense, not devices to throw and pin people.

During the worst fighting of World War II, Ueshiba declared:

The Way of the Warrior has been misunderstood as a means to kill and destroy others. Those who seek competition are making a grave mistake. To smash, injure, or destroy is the worst sin a human being can commit. The real Way of the Warrior is to prevent slaughter. It is the Art of Peace, the Power of Love.

It is this concern for the opponent that makes Aikido radically different from other martial arts. Two ancient concepts of *budo* are *ai nuke*, "mutual preservation," and *katsu jin ken*, "the saving of your enemy's life." Both imply choice, action, and *responsibility*. This is a difficult way, an internal spiritual discipline, that offers neither the thrill of justified vengeance and murder nor the congratulatory self-righteousness of passivism.

Aikido even redefines the idea of "enemy" or "opponent." It is the only martial art recommended by counselors of parents of *abusive children*. Imagine a small or aged parent whose 17-year-old 200-pound star fullback son or grandson comes home drunk and dangerous. By law the parent is responsible — *yet there must be no harm to the child*. The same dilemma of care and concern in a potentially dangerous situation has left many a strong man helpless.

Many karate students walk into the dojo, watch for a few minutes, decide "it's faking" and walk back out. One night came a young man with a black belt in Tae Kwon Do — and a problem. His fraternity brothers were coming home roaring drunk, throwing punches and kicks to get him to show them "his moves" never realizing (perhaps) that his karate was designed to break ribs and smash throats. "What can I do?" he asked. "These are my brothers. I don't want to hurt them." His care, compassion, and unwillingness to harm were getting him beaten up. We showed him *tenkan*, a "turning of the other cheek" that protects all. He stayed.

Aikido is designed to *control* rather than *destroy* the opponent. The Aikidoist does not punch or kick to injure, does not block or resist attacks but blends with, redirects and *transforms* the attacker's energy through use of movement and *ki*.

Shin-Shin Toitsu Aikido is the style of Aikido founded by Ueshiba's student Koichi Tohei in 1974. It means "Aikido with Mind-Body Coordinated" and differs from other styles primarily in the *formalized* study of *ki* development and *ki* testing. This provides an unusual opportunity to actually test, measure, and evaluate concepts of mind and spirit which otherwise must be dismissed as "flaky New Age weirdness" or accepted on faith, despite doubts or fears.

What is Ki?

Some think of *ki* as the universal spirit present in all things. This seemingly exotic concept has much in common with the ancient Hebrew *ruach,* meaning "smoke," "wind," or "spirit"[1] and with the ancient Greek *pneuma* meaning "air," "breath," or "spirit."

The Greek word is familiar in modern English pertaining to air or other gases, or their mechanical properties. But the older, deeper meaning is the animating breath of life — the spirit. In the original Greek of the New Testament of the Bible, the word appearing in English as "spirit" or "soul" is actually one of two Greek words — *psyche* (also meaning "life" and equivalent to the Latin *anima*) or *pneuma.* And our English *spirit* is from the Latin *spiritus,* literally meaning "breath" (as in *respiration,* "breath-ing").

> *God* [Theos] *is a spirit* [pneuma].
>
> *— John 4:24*

> *The* wind *[pneuma] blows wherever it pleases. You may hear its sound, but you cannot tell where it comes from or where it is going. So it is with everyone born* of the Spirit *[pneumatos].*
>
> *— John 3:8*

"Harmonious ki" or *aiki* may also be thought of as "that which is right." Sometimes it is *"aiki"* (right) to fall or fail, or to cause an opponent to fall or fail, but "not *aiki"* to add punishment to action. This moves you from the negative trap of revenge thinking, the neutral of retribution, to the positive of control or constraint for the sake of all concerned, to accord with what is right.

---

[1] "If we may trust to language," noted Freud (*Moses and Monotheism, 1938)* "it was the movement of the air that provided the image of spirituality, since the spirit borrows its name from the breath of wind (*animus, spiritus,* Hebrew: *ruach,* smoke)." Hence the "cloths hung in groves" (referred to in the Old Testament of the Bible) were essentially serving as "spirit" detectors.

This accord, harmony, softness and relaxation is not weakness nor is gentleness passivity. Care and concern for the attacker is not mere sentimentality nor does it lessen effectiveness.

Dave Butts was a devastating All-Pro defensive tackle for the Washington Redskins football team. His job was to knock down the opposing quarterback, and he did it very well. But watching Butts and his quarry go down, you would often see him slip an arm under his opponent's helmet to cushion the fall; or roll so that his body (300-some pounds) would not come down on top of the other player. Contrast this approach with that of players who delight in body slamming their opponents.

Nonaka Sensei of Hawaii presents a highly practical reason for not bashing the opponent: "He will not be happy." None of us can afford to fill the world with people who feel they have something to avenge.

Aikido offers an unusual combination of care and effectiveness. Wise kindness. Tough love.

The Concept of "Reality"

Ki can also be defined as "attention" or "mind." While the concept of "extending *ki*" is vitally important in Aikido, what it actually is that you are extending is not so important. A strong case can be made for "it doesn't matter" *if* the end result is the same, *if* the final results are real. Beginners have difficulties with this concept. I, like many others, wasted at least six months debating whether what I was seeing was "real" or "not real." Experience won.

To some, the challenge of believing in the existence of *ki* is the challenge of believing in the existence of the spirit. The reality of things unseen sometimes poses severe difficulties for Westerners.[2]

If the idea of extending a beam of energy from your fingers out to the edge of the cosmos violates your sense of reality, then think of it as "attention" or "mind" and use this concept as a working hypothesis, a tool, as did Einstein riding his hypothetical beam of light. If this *were* true, what *would* you see? What *would* happen?

Did Einstein "really" go riding on a beam of light? Not in the usual sense, but the thought was "real" in that it produced "real" results. He was able to see using this image and what he saw is now considered very real indeed.

If you send your mind to the core of the earth so that anyone trying to move you must move the planet, are you really physically attached to millions of tons of rock? Not in the usual sense, but if the thought results in real stability and real power and your opponent really can't budge you, how is this *un-real*?

---

[2] Perhaps this is why the man known as *Yeshua*, or *Jesus*, or *Christ,* chose for his disciples sailors, *men who could see the wind.*

Images and Visualization

The exercises in this *Sampler* contain a variety of images. In *Aikido*, just as in gymnastics, dance, or golf, the image is a vital part of the technique; we create the image in the mind then let the body catch up. Imaging helps or allows the body to move, react, or feel in ways that may not be possible when working from the purely intellectual.[3]

In Aikido, a common image is that of water. Water flows yet is incompressible. It is soft and yielding but also produces the rock-hardness of the firehose. Water can carve the rock, shape the coastline, bathe the child.

Be a water drop. Be a wave flowing *over* and around a rock or rolling in and out from the shore. Be a leaf in the water floating with the current. Play with the images until you have learned the *feeling* that the images invoke — then reproduce that feeling.

Visualization and *ki* extension raise the startling possibilities that our thoughts do become reality on some level. Yet *ki* does not violate the laws of physics; it allows physical actions to move and flow more freely. In a strictly physical sense, holding a certain image in your mind may allow tiny physical adjustments — a slight shift in weight, a slight rounding of the chest, a faint drop in the shoulders, the use or relaxation of certain muscles — to occur on an unconscious level which would be far more difficult on a conscious level. It may produce an equally important change in attitude, in our perception of limits and boundaries.

---

[3] In the 60's, instructions for dancing "The Twist" were reduced to the following: "Dry your bottom with a bathtowel while rubbing out a cigarette with your toe." Complex coordination of movements was immediately possible when translated into these familiar images.

What Is One-Point?

At least part of what Aikidoists call the One-Point, center, or *hara*, is what physicists call the "center of gravity, the point where gravity acts on the body as a whole." When the normal human stands upright in a normal posture, the center of mass is approximately between the spine and the navel. The vertical location of the One-Point is commonly said to be about two inches below the navel. If you fold your hands in front of you and drop them to your abdomen, your little fingers will be approximately at your One-Point — sometimes.

Actually, the One-Point is not a rigid, precisely defined point nor is it to be "kept" in its place. It is in different places in people of different size and body build and it is in different places in one person depending on what that person is doing in the sense of dynamic equilibrium. It may even be outside of the body.

A standing immobile body is stable as long as the One-Point remains over its support — the feet. If the center of mass moves outside of its support (the feet) gravity pulling on that point creates an imbalance. An additional tug by the tiniest person can produce spectacular results.

Testing for One-Point and Ki

Shin-Shin Toitsu Aikido emphasizes coordination of mind and body to produce inner strength and stability. A person with mind and body coordinated conveys an image of indefinable calmness and stability. *Ki* testing defines that state of calmness and stability through exercises known as *ki tests*. Although it is impossible to test the mind directly, the mind can be tested through the body.

The point of testing is not to see if *uke* (the tester) can defeat *nage* (the one performing the technique). *Ki* testing is not a physical contest but a demonstration of *nage*'s current state of mind-body coordination. *Uke* serves as a biofeedback sensor to aid *nage* in learning new concepts of strength, and calmness, and stability. This relationship between mind and body, body and spirit is the secret behind Aikido and other martial arts. It even offers a testable, sensible rationale for positive, creative, everyday living.

Exercises are grouped according to these basic rules for practice of Mind-Body Coordination. This arrangement is somewhat artificial as all of these principles work together. With any one of the principles you can pass any *ki* test; on losing any one of the principles, you can fail any *ki* test.

Rules For Mind-Body Coordination

Each of the rules below is a natural extension of the one before.

1. Keep One-Point
2. Relax completely
3. Keep weight underside
4. Extend *ki*.

What You're Really Looking For

Not necessarily spectacular strength, or dramatic failure, just *a difference*. Perhaps a tiny, subtle increase in firmness. A slightly longer period of resistance. Perhaps no difference to *uke*, but less effort by *nage* to maintain stability.

Uke can increase the challenge in small increments as *nage* learns and improves until the differences are spectacular indeed. Because a strong *nage* may easily resist the efforts of a physically weaker *uke* without resorting to anything faintly resembling the point of the exercise, partners should be of approximately equal physical strength or the stronger partner must take care to be particularly sensitive. Testing should never deteriorate into a wrestling match.

Ki testing is a teaching tool, not an attack (for which we would use Aikido techniques). A fierce rush of mass and motion is not dealt with only by extending *ki* unless there is no other option available. If, for example, a large oncoming mass has *Mack* emblazoned across the grill, we do not stand in the middle of the road extending *ki*; ideally, we extend *ki* — and step aside.

Does it really work? Try it and see.

Believe nothing, O monks, merely because you have been told it. Do not believe what your teacher tells you merely out of respect for the teacher. But whatsoever, after due examination and analysis, you find to be kind, conducive to the good, the benefit, the welfare of all beings — that doctrine believe and cling to, and take it as your guide.

— Buddha

It's Really Just ...

Programming

Ki testing is sometimes dismissed by baffled onlookers as mere "programming" or some form of hypnosis. It is actually a means of revealing previous programming for what it is. Our minds are programmed with astonishing ease. Don't believe it?

1. Ask a friend or a group to repeat aloud: 10, 10, 10, 10, 10, 10, 10, 10, 10, 10, 10, 10.

   Ask this question: "What are aluminum cans made of?"

   (Next question: "So what are *tin* cans made of?")

2. Ask a friend or a group to repeat aloud: "Pots, pots, pots, pots, pots, pots, pots."

   Ask this question: "What do you do at a green light?"

   (Next question: "So what do you do at a *red* light?")

3. What does F - O - L - K spell?

   What is the word that means *to feed a fire*?

   What is the word for the white part of an egg?

You can program or be programmed to weaken yourself with negative self-defeating thoughts as easily as you just programmed someone else to think that aluminum cans are made of tin, that we stop at a green lights, or that white is yellow.

Whether you think you can or think you can't, you're right.

— Henry Ford

Supernatural Powers

The distinction between *natural* and *supernatural* is so often misused and misunderstood that it is useful to look at the words.

Super (from Latin) means "over" or "above" or "higher." *Natural* (from Latin *natus*, past participle of *nasci*, to be born) means "as born" hence the kinds of skills and abilities which we expect most normal people to have or not to have.

In *common* usage, however,

- [ ] *Natural* means: "We are familiar with this."
- [ ] *Supernatural* means:

    —"we don't believe this exists" or

    —"we don't understand this phenomenon" or

    —"we don't have a mechanism that explains how this observable but disturbing phenomenon might operate."

Properly used, the term *supernatural power* should refer to:

Any ability above or beyond those that standard human beings appear to be "born" with.

Things appear "supernatural" when understanding is lacking or incomplete. But fact is fact, and power is power, whether we understand it or not.

We are "born" with far more than we sometimes realize. A newborn can put an amazingly strong grip on your finger despite being a tiny "weak" baby. Most beginners can perform basic *ki* exercises in seconds — it is only when they start thinking about it, doubting it, "knowing" that it is impossible, that their ability starts to waver and weaken to the point that they must relearn what they already knew how to do the day they walked in.

Truth 101: Truth is that which is true — whether you know it or not and whether you like it or not.

— Ben Swett

Faking

So if not "programming" or weird "supernatural powers" the results of testing must be fakery, pure and simple. Well, they can be. That is why you must always *test the tester*.

It is very easy to unconsciously (or consciously) change the force, direction, or other characteristic of the test to obtain a desired end. Having fallen into any one of these temptations, *uke* may have made his point, but has not performed a true *ki* test — *he did not test what he claimed to be testing*.

The flip side of this problem is the *nage* who "knows" he is supposed to "be weak" under particular conditions or "be strong" under others and so collapses or stands firm according to script. This makes for great theater but it is not *ki* testing.

It is also tempting for *nage* to counter the expected energy ("Ha-ha, you can't get me!") This is why every Aikido technique works about twice with beginners. As one of the worst all-time offenders in this category, I can say that this is a profound misunderstanding of the nature and purpose of *ki* testing. *Ki* testing is not a contest, but an *evaluation* in which *uke* has kindly consented to serve as a biofeedback detector of *nage*'s internal state.

To avoid any of these situations, test several times to experiment with the technique, the feeling, and observable results. Then repeat the tests *with nage choosing the conditions — but without telling uke*. Then verify results of *nage*'s internal choices with *uke*'s external observations. For example,

1. *Nage* thinks of a co-worker he dislikes. *Uke* test.
2. *Nage* thinks of an especially happy day. *Uke* test.
3. *Nage* chooses to think of one or the other. *Uke* test.
4. From the results *uke* tries to guess which topic or what combination of the two *nage* was thinking of. *Nage* then confirms or does not confirm *uke's* conclusion.

This approach removes all temptation for *uke* to load or skew the test in any way and provides essential reality testing for *nage*.

Test Lists

Shin-Shin Toitsu Do Test List for Ki Development

Sho Kyu (Over 10 years old) Test 1

1. Standing (one foot forward) See "Hanmi" on page 32.
2. Unbendable Arm. See "Unbendable Arm*" on page 18 and on page 100.
3. Thrusting out one hand with weight underside. See Unraisable Arm* on page 90.
4. Sitting *seiza*. See "Sitting Seiza*" on page 21.
5. Sitting down and standing up.

Chu Kyu (Over 13 years old) , Sho kyu Test 2, Chu kyu Test 1

6. Sitting cross-legged while being pushed from behind, while being raised by one knee. See "Sitting Cross-Legged" on page 23.
7. Thrusting out one hand, then being pushed by the wrist. See "Wrist Push*" on page 60.
8. Bending backward.
9. Stooping.
10. Unraisable Body. See "Unliftable Body*" on page 92.

Jo Kyu Test 1 (Over 15 years old), Shokyu Test 3, Chu Kyu Test 2

11. Leaning backward on a partner. See "Leaning Backward*" on page 56.
12. Leaning forward on a partner. See "Leaning Forward*" on page 57.
13. Thrusting out one hand and raising one leg. See "Wrist Push*" on page 60.
14. Holding up both hands. See "Raising Arms*" on page 58.
15. Walking forward when being held. See "Ki Door" on page 103.
16. Sitting cross-legged, being pushed from the front by two hands. See "Sitting Cross-Legged*" on page 22.
17. Sitting *seiza* while being given a two-way test. See "Rotation*" on page 49.
18. Sitting *seiza* and bowing forward while being held from the rear by both shoulders. See "Bowing*" on page 72.

Hitori Waza — Ki Testing for Aikido

Ki testing for rank in Aikido is separate from *Shin-Shin Toitsu Do* tests for *Ki* Development. Items listed below appear in this *Sampler* as "exercises" (*undo*). On the tests they appear as "techniques" (*waza*) as they are critical components of the Aikido throws.

Requirements for 5th *Kyu* (the first adult level) through 2nd *Kyu* are given here. Testing for 1st *Kyu* (Brown Belt) comprises all listed items plus the Six-Count *Jo Taigi*, *Jo Taigi 1*, and *Jo Taigi 22*.

5th Kyu

Udemawashi Waza. See "Arm Dropping" on page 87.
Udefuri Waza. See "Arm Swinging*" on page 70.
Udefuri-Choyaku Waza. See "Spinning*" on page 71.
Sayu Waza.
Ushiro-Ukemi Waza. See "Rolling Backwards and Forwards*" on page 25.
Zenpo-Kaiten Waza. See "Cross-Rolls*" on page 30.
Taigi 5.

4th Kyu — All previous tests plus:

Ikkyo Waza. See "Ikkyo-Undo" on page 131.
Zengo Waza. See "Two-Direction Exercise" on page 134.
Happo Waza. See "Eight-Way Exercise" on page 135.
Zenshin-Koshin Waza.
Taigi 15.

3rd Kyu — All previous tests plus:

Funekogi Waza.
Nikyo Waza.
Sankyo Waza. See "Sankyo" on page 108.
Kote-Gaeshi Waza.

Second Kyu — All previous tests plus:

Kaho Tekubi-Kosa Waza.
Joho Tekubi-Kosa Waza.
Ushiro-Tori Waza.
Ushiro Tekubi-Tori Zenshin Waza.
Ushiro Tekubi-Tori Koshin Waza.

The Basics

The following techniques — sitting, rolling, standing, turning, and Unbendable Arm — are the positions or exercises commonly subjected to *ki* testing. That is, you may perform a *ki* test by checking a person's stability while sitting, standing, or recovering from a turn or roll or by checking for Unbendable Arm.

Unbendable Arm*

In this classic exercise, *uke* tries to bend *nage*'s extended arm at the elbow while *nage* keeps the arm strong but *relaxed,* extending *ki* and attention beyond the arm. *Uke* tests gently at first with steadily increasing challenge as *nage* learns the feel. Once learned, *nage* will be able to maintain Unbendable Arm, exhibiting a strength beyond all apparent physical capacity.

A smaller or weaker *uke* may test *nage*'s Unbendable Arm by placing *nage's* hand on his shoulder then placing his own hands on *nage*'s elbow joint and dropping weight underside. If there is a serious height difference, the taller partner may kneel or sit.

To help the feeling, *nage* may:

a)   Imagine a water pump in the abdomen that pumps water up through the torso, through the arm and out the fingers.

b)   Imagine touching the opposite wall of the room.

c)   Reach out to touch the index finger of a third person.

Unbendable Arm illustrates extension, the power of a goal outside the immediate battlefield (the elbow), and the weakness of tension and fixation.

This exercise also illustrates the common misunderstanding of what strength really is and what it really is not.

Strength is not tension.

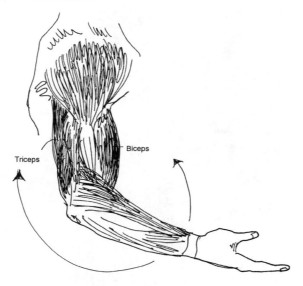

From a purely muscular (and simplified) standpoint, two antagonistic muscles are involved in Unbendable Arm: *biceps brachii* and *triceps brachii*. *Biceps* flexes (bends) the arm, while *triceps* extends (straightens) it. Keeping the arm extended while *uke* tries to bend it requires only *triceps*.

If *biceps* is tense and tight during this exercise, energy is being diverted to fighting *triceps*; you are fighting yourself. *Uke* or a third partner can help by checking the tension of the *biceps* muscle during the course of the exercise.

Sitting

Sitting Seiza*

Seiza ("correct-sitting") is the formal Japanese sitting or kneeling posture. Because it can be uncomfortable for beginners with tight leg muscles or for those with bad knees, students may sit cross-legged or on a *seiza* stool (a slant-top stool as shown) or on a chair. These positions tend not to be as stable, however, so *uke* must be especially sensitive while testing.

From a kneeling position,

☐ Forehead and weight of head are over One-Point rather than over the feet.

☐ Lower back curves gently in.

☐ Hands rest lightly on the thighs.

☐ Right big toe is over left big toe.

☐ Posture is softly erect.

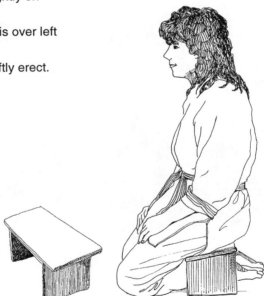

When pressure is applied to the chest (with mind and body coordinated) *seiza* allows you to transfer the force to the tailbone which, being pushed into the mat, just makes you more stable.

Sitting Cross-Legged*

Cross-legged sitting is more comfortable and familiar for the beginner than *seiza*. Shoulders are relaxed, weight slightly forward and hands rest on knees slightly forward of ankles. Weight is properly distributed when it is difficult for a partner to lift the knee.

This position is inherently less stable than *seiza* because the pelvis is more rounded. It flows very naturally, however, into a backwards roll.

Rolling*

"On the street," a favorite phrase in martial arts classes, *usually* means "in the movies" or "as seen on TV." Yes, we live in a violent world but studies have repeatedly shown that those who watch TV regularly have a severely warped view of the world and see it as a far more dangerous, violent place than it really is. They feel more helpless, hostile, and fearful of neighbors and strangers than those who deal with the real world and real people. But feelings of helplessness, hostility, and fear, whatever their source, feed the cycle of fear and violence.

In our Fairfax County recreation classes, we regularly found that most students had signed up for self-defense "on the street." Students attracted to the county classes by the advertisement of a "non-violent martial art" enjoyed themselves and each other. A new martial arts film, however, always seemed to bring an influx of terrified and hostile students.[4]

"Who has *ever* actually been personally threatened on the street?" we asked. Over three years and nearly 200 students, there were only three and all had dealt successfully with the problem.

"Who has tripped over feet or curb anytime in the last month?" All hands went up. What then, is the most practical form of "self-defense" with the most immediate value?

Rolls are hands-free. Note that the most common injuries "on the street" are from attempting to break a fall (and breaking a wrist instead). Rolls are circular (we use breakfalls only rarely). Once the technique and dynamics of rolling have been mastered it doesn't really matter whether the "wheel" of your body rolls over a mat or over a parking lot.

The ability to fall and roll safely is one of the best self-defense techniques there is. But as usual in Aikido, there's more to it

"We learn to roll," says Sensei George Simcox, "so that we can help someone else to learn Aikido."

---

[4] "On the road," is a little different; see "The Gridlock." And some areas of our country are worse than war zones. See also "Radio and TV."

Rolling Backwards and Forwards*

This is a simple rolling back and forth (*koho-tento-undo*) like a rocking chair.

Sitting cross-legged with hands on thighs,

1. At count of One, roll backwards by rounding the lower back.

2. On count of Two, roll forward to original position.

The roll begins by rounding the lower back, not by flinging back the head. Throwing the head back puts the head in an unsafe position. Be a ball, not a brick. To keep back rounded during the roll, think of touching knee to nose or look at your belt.

Hands remain on knees or thighs; they do not touch the mat.

Rolling Backwards and Rising to a Kneel

Roll back as in previous exercise, but on coming forward,

1. Tuck the near leg as close to the pelvis as possible.

2. Bring other leg forward, bent at an angle of up to (but not greater than) ninety degrees. By pushing off with the tucked back leg (*not* with hands),

3. Rise into a kneeling position with back leg at an oblique angle to the body. (You can't roll with back leg perpendicular to the body).

From here, it is easy to drop back to another backward roll or rise to a standing position (see *hanmi* on page 32).

Tempted to use hands? Clap them.

Back Rolls

A complete back roll continues the motion of the backward-forward roll. To do a complete back roll,

1. Start from the kneeling position, left foot forward and left knee up, right knee and leg on the mat at an oblique angle to the body.

2. Look at your left knee. You will be "throwing" this left knee over your left shoulder.

3. Look right, rock back and sit down past the mat leg while throwing your left leg over your left shoulder. As hips go overhead, continue the motion by pushing off with left arm.

4. As you complete the roll, bring your left leg forward to the original starting position.

Forward Rolls*

Forward rolls are more complex than back rolls — and painful if improperly done. For this reason, It is highly recommended that you get formal instruction from an Aikido *dojo*.

Kneeling with left knee on mat, right knee up,

1. Lean forward placing right Unbendable Arm with back of right hand on mat. (Or join hands forming arms into a large circle).

2. Tuck and turn neck and head away from the rolling arm (left).

3. Curving back, neck and arm into a large circle, push off with toes, move hips forward rolling along right hand and arm and across back.

4. End in a kneel or standing (*hanmi*).

The Aikido roll (unlike the tumbling roll taught in schools) does not flip over, but rolls slightly sideways *down* the arm, *across* the back to the hip. The head is tucked away from the rolling arm. This roll protects the nape of the neck and the spine so well that, properly done, it makes no difference whether you are rolling on a mat or on concrete.

A hard painful thump at the small of the back or hip means you are not tucking enough. Think of touching your knee to your nose or look at your belt while rolling to maintain roundness.

Students often try rolls or other techniques two or three times and when all does not work perfectly, conclude that it's "too hard."

Traditionally the beginning jujitsu student was given an assignment: one thousand rolls.

After doing one thousand rolls you will know how to roll. And you will no longer be a beginner.

Cross-Rolls*

Cross rolls (*zempo-kaiten waza*) are done as in normal forward rolls, but begin with left knee up and right arm on mat.

The *Aikido* test list (*Hitori waza*) requires a series of three of these small rolls done in series while maintaining the same arm/leg relationships. Beginners who are hopelessly confused between right and left sometimes find it helpful to practice by tying a string around the big toe or by putting a sock on the "rolling" foot.

During rolling practice, students are sometimes challenged to see who can travel the length of the mat with the *fewest* large rolls, and who can do it with the *most* small rolls.

Hot tip: cross-rolls are the answer to the "most rolls" problem.

Standing Rolls

Standing rolls are essentially the same as small rolls and end in *hanmi*, the standing position (see page 32).

Standing Backward Rolls

Standing backward rolls are done just as small backward rolls from the kneeling position except that you first place the top of the foot on the mat, drop to the kneeling position and roll from there.

Standing Forward Rolls

Standing forward rolls are done in the same way as small forward rolls except that you must roll along a larger circle which extends out further from your beginning position. See this and get training before you try it.

Standing — Hanmi

Hanmi is the standing position.

To rise into *hanmi* from a kneeling position,

1. Push off with legs only (no hands!)
2. With left foot forward, right foot back, rise up on toes.
3. Lower heels to floor without moving weight backwards.
4. Stand comfortably, with attention at One-Point.

Hanmi (meaning "half-body") comes from Japanese sword tradition. It is a deceptively and astonishingly stable position. The

distance between front and back foot is quite small. Stability comes from mind-body coordination and One-Point, not just the geometry of foot position.

Left hanmi means standing in this position with the left foot forward. *Right hanmi* means standing in this position with the right foot forward.

Hanmi looks unthreatening, even casual and unconcerned, but offers dynamic stability, ease of motion — and you can dance to it.

This statement is not as frivolous as might appear. The classic karate stances are intended to provide a solid platform for outgoing punches and kicks, and a brace against incoming force. The Aikidoist simply moves out of the way, and can do so easily.

Karate instructors constantly told me to <u>widen</u> my stance.

Aikido instructors constantly urged me to <u>narrow</u> it.

— CMS

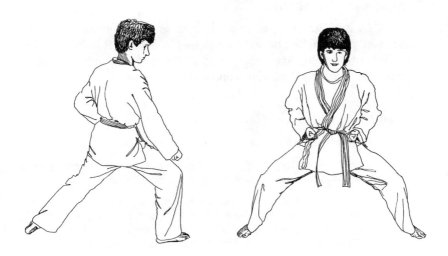

To test this, try a waltz around the room with one partner in *hanmi*, one in horse-stance (the karate stance shown at right).

Which partner can move more easily?

Tenkan (Turning)*

A *tenkan* is a "turning," a simple maneuver that is, in fact, one of the most powerful and devastating moves in Aikido. It is the Aikido version of "turning the other cheek." Balance and direction are extremely important and a common subject of *ki* testing.

In left *hanmi* (left foot and left hand forward)

1. *Uke* seizes *nage*'s left wrist with the right hand.

   (Grasp gently to provide a pivot point and a point of reference rather than an exercise in breaking a death grip.)

2. *Nage* curls fingers and wrist back towards palm, then steps or slides forward with the left foot, pivoting 180 degrees to end up approximately shoulder to shoulder with *uke* or slightly behind. Draw the left foot back as necessary.

   Left foot is still forward and right foot back (still in left *hanmi*).

Once the motion is learned, *nage* can practice alone by:

a) Pivoting around his own extended hand (alternating right and left hands) or around a staff

b) Turning in place or

c) Turning every few steps while walking.

Turning the other cheek is a form of moral ju-jitsu.

— *Rev. Gerald Stanley Lee*
1862 - 1944

In 1982, I gleefully demonstrated a karate technique for breaking a hold to and on my "Old Swordmaster" Ben Swett. He demonstrated tenkan. I couldn't see it, didn't understand what he had just done or what he was talking about. All he had done was turn around. So? "I think," he said, "that you would enjoy Aikido." He was right.

— CMS

Testing Technique

Nage may stand or sit.

1.   *Uke* stands or sits in *seiza* perpendicular to *nage* (the partner who will take the test).

2.   With the palm or fingers of the hand nearest *nage*'s chest, *uke* applies pressure to *nage's* chest, perpendicular to *nage*'s chest, fingers parallel to the floor. Pressure is applied until *nage* begins to lose stability.

3.   *Uke* observes the amount of effort required to disrupt stability.

This configuration is for beginning *nages and* for beginning *ukes* tempted to approach the exercise as a contest; less mechanical advantage makes it harder for *uke* to bowl over his partner. *Uke's* fingers are parallel to the mat because the hand tends to follow the fingers. A test done with fingers directed upwards tends to go in that direction — very difficult. Testing is divided into three levels.

Test One

Test One is the basic test for beginners. *Nage* tests with gentle or gradually increasing pressure.

Test Two

Test Two, a slightly more advanced test, is applied in *nage*'s sight with a hesitation.

Uke may bring a hand in rapidly as if to punch, stop, then proceed with the test.

Or, *uke* may place a hand a few inches away from *nage*'s body and wait to see if *nage* withdraws or moves toward the hand in anticipation (see "Magnetic Hand" on page 38).

Test Three

Test Three is testing with *ki*.

Nage must extend *ki* out in all directions so that *uke*'s *ki* never even enters *nage*'s body.

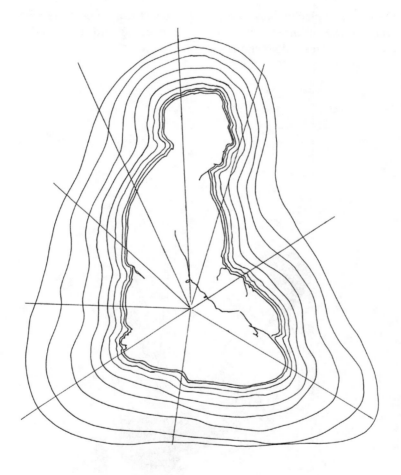

Magnetic Hand

Beginners commonly approach *ki* testing by leaning into the test in an attempt to increase mechanical advantage, especially if *uke* hesitates before testing (Test Two). This is the notorious "Magnetic Hand" — *uke* holds it out and *nage* is attracted to it like magic.

Unfortunately, you cannot improve stability just by rocking forward because you end up rocking back and lose stability. Also, the test criterion of "perpendicular to *nage*'s body" becomes "up" — a far more difficult test. Or, *nage* may be tested *during* a motion rather than *after* the motion has been completed.

The cure for Magnetic Hand is for *uke* to immediately test *from the rear* and for *nage* to purposely do this a few times to see that it doesn't work.

Rather than a lean forward, try a bunny hop forward. This changes the environment but not the posture.

Variations

The possibilities are endless, but include the following tests.

With *nage* in *seiza*:

a) Pressing from front (chest) and back.

b) Pressing shoulder from the side.

c) Lifting *nage's* knee.

d) Lifting hand (not straight up from knee, but pushing hand towards shoulder).

With *nage* standing,

a) Pressing from front (chest), back, and small of back.

b) Pressing shoulder from the side.

c) Lifting *nage's* leg from ankle.

d) Unbendable Arm.

Keep One-Point

Keep One-Point

One-Point is thought of as a point within the abdomen, several inches below the naval. The Chinese know it as the *tan-t'ien*, the "sea of *ch'i*." The Dugum Dani of New Guinea talk of the *edai egen*, or "seed of singing," as the source of life power at the center of the body. In English we talk of someone with spirit and fortitude as having "guts."

In Japanese, this point is known as the *hara*[5], the center of life and spiritual energy, a point-source of light and *ki*. In keeping with the Japanese tradition, the Aikidoist thinks of One-Point as *the* central point. We drop weight underside, to One-Point. We relax, focusing on One-Point. We extend *ki* from One-Point.

An attack and a reaction both have a rhythm and a beat. Since Aikido movement begins at the One-point and is detected by the One-Point, Aikido technique has a music, a rhythm of its own. Sensei Susan Chandler, whose workshops emphasize music and rhythm, thinks of One-Point as the "conductor" of the music of the body.

On the mat, we constantly test for One-Point. From the strictly physical standpoint, One-Point is the body's center of gravity, the center point of rotation. Good balance depends on good One-Point and everything else in physical technique depends on that. Focus on this point is called "having One-Point" or simply "One-Point." A shift or loss of One-Point can be as obvious as a fall or it can be extremely subtle requiring the assistance of *uke* to help detect its loss or misplacement.

In high-speed sports such as skiing or skating, a shift in One-Point at speeds up to 20 or 60 miles per hour can be more immediately obvious (wear protective gear!) than at "normal mat speeds." The tiniest shift produces remarkable results. Too far forward and your strokes will lose all power or you will go into a nose dive. Too far back and feet will fly up into a dangerous backward flip. Although it seems reasonable to lean forward while skating up a hill, it is always best to stay centered over One-Point. Eventually the skater

---

[5] The *hara* is familiar in English (badly garbled) as "harry-karry," ritual suicide committed by a cut (*kiri*) to the abdomen and the *hara*.

discovers that power and speed come not by stroking with the feet but by shifting of the One-Point. One begins to feel less like a runner on wheels and more like a pendulum; One-Point is the center of rotation.

This dynamic stability is seen in several familiar children's toys. The Punching Doll, when struck, rotates around its One-Point to return to its original position.[6] In Japan, such dolls (*daruma*) symbolize good luck, or at least persistence — the ability to keep coming back again and again despite adversity.

As a toy, the gyroscope is a highly stable spinning top. In engineering it provides a stable reference point for navigation, helping to stabilize and direct ships and planes.

In Aikido, the One-Point offers the same stabilizing effect. It is thought of not only as the center of the body but of the universe. The idea is that since the universe is infinite, its center can be *anywhere* — so it may as well be at your One-Point — and for me, the center of the universe may as well be at mine. Whether physical or non-physical, this location can be placed and shifted through mind and attitude.

Although we relax, drop weight underside and extend *ki*, we must always come back to One-Point.

Maxine Wright recounts a story told by a retired military officer who, as an inexperienced young man, was so fascinated by the sight of his troops marching to his command that he didn't think to call them back until they were well out of earshot. The situation was rescued by his lieutenant.

Regardless of the beautiful throw, the long soaring soccer kick, despite good fortune or adversity, keep One-Point.

---

[6] Application of the same principles to the statues of Easter Island resolved centuries of myth and mystery surrounding the Stone-Age transport of 10- to 40-ton stone giants over many miles of rough terrain. See Heyerdahl (1989).

The Goldfish Bowl

For smoother rolling,

1. Imagine a goldfish bowl in your pelvis filled with water or a glowing, liquid, white light.

2. Roll and stand and move in such a way that you do not splash the water or disturb the fish.

Rubber Band

A visualization for stable rolling.

1. *Nage* rolls backward and forward (*koho tento-undo*).

2. *Uke* tests as *nage* returns to stable sitting position.

3. *Nage* imagines a rubber band stretching from One-Point or chest to the opposite wall. *Uke* test.

Test One: *uke* waits until *nage* has settled into position.

Test Two: *uke* tests as *nage* is still coming up.

Student: "But all I did was change what I was thinking."
Instructor: "Yes."

— *G. Ford-Kohne*

Moving One-Point

While sitting in *seiza*, cross-legged, or standing, *nage* places mind in different positions:

a) At the test point (*uke*'s hand).

b) On top of the head.

c) At the center of the earth.

d) At One-Point.

e) On the big toe.

f) Across the room.

Uke test on request. Compare stability of different placements.

With *nage* in *seiza*, having established One-Point,

1. *Uke* runs a finger up *nage*'s spine like a zipper.

2. *Uke* test.

A classic means of disrupting stability is to tap nage on the head or tousle the hair. These are the ki-test equivalents of tennis players who stop play to ask you to show exactly where you put your thumb on the racket, or the losing volleyball team that loudly announces to the winning server that this serve is for Game Point. Practice maintaining One-Point in spite of these attempts by uke to move One-Point for you.

"Say One-Point"

After you have begun to master the concept and practice of locating and keeping One-Point,

1. *Nage* say "One-Point" while raising arm. *Uke* test.

2. *Nage* say "One-Point" *then* raise arm. *Uke* Test.

The challenge is to raise the arm while leaving mind at One-Point. Test may be Unbendable Arm or any other test.

An easy way to do this is to allow the arms to rise on their own as if floating in water. Try something many of us did as children.

Standing in a doorway, press the backs of both hands as hard as possible against the frame. Now, relax and step outside the frame. The arms will rise — and be Unbendable as well.

Rotation*

An exercise in absorbing physical energy *internally*. In *seiza*,

1. *Uke* pushes *nage* on front of chest.

2. *Uke* pushes *nage's* shoulder from the side.

3. *Uke* combines the two tests, pushing from the front then adding a gentle push from the side.

This is one of the most difficult of the basic ki tests. A helpful image is some version of this: sitting on a swing, a little red wagon, or a platform on casters welcoming a push because the harder the push uke gives, the better the ride. Wheee!

But the push is all handled internally allowing the external body to remain still.

Words

Words are not "just semantics"[7] but powerful tools and weapons.

"Squeezing" vs. "Fisting"

1. *Uke* offer a hand and asks *nage* to "squeeze" as hard as possible.
2. Without changing position, *uke* ask *nage* to "make a fist."
3. *Uke* compare the forces generated by the two actions.

"Squeeze" is a somewhat indefinite command with many options but we all know what it means "to make a fist."

George Simcox tells of Mary Anne Brown who seemingly could not learn "Unraisable Arm." Finally, instead of telling her to "put" the arm out there, George said "place" the arm. She stood strong. The change in one little word made all the difference.

"Try" vs. "Do"

Test the following progression. *Nage* say each of these aloud.

1. I *can't* keep Unbendable Arm.
2. I will *try* to keep Unbendable Arm.
3. I will *keep* Unbendable Arm.
4. The arm is Unbendable.

Countless lectures and sermons have been preached on the negative effects of "can't" but note that "try" is little different as it has in it the built-in possibility of failure. Look for other examples of effects by words that are far more than "just semantics." Words signify radically different things to different people. See Elgin, Suzette (1980).

---

[7] From Gr. *sêmantikos*, having significance, from *sêmantos*, marked, from *sêmainein*, to signify, from *sêma*, a sign, not "just" a sign, but something of very real and distinct importance.

Changing Size

In a grab, you typically want to become smaller, enabling yourself to move with ease within *uke*'s grasp, within your own skin. Combine this exercise with "Letting Go" on page 81.

Nage imagine:

1. Growing down below the mat and up to the ceiling. *Uke* test.

2. Expanding to fit the confines of the room, then beyond, becoming the size of the earth, extending to the ends of the universe. *Uke* test the effect of various images.

    See Breathing and Meditation. See also the video "Powers of Ten" under Books, Movies, and Videos.

Cats have loose skin, as does the Rhodesian Ridgeback, a dog used for hunting lions. Both these animals are remarkably able to move within their skin should it become caught in claws.

Horses are notorious for deep breathing exercises when being saddled against their will; no matter how tightly the cinch is pulled, breathing out loosens it.

Be at least as wise as a cat or dog or horse — don't get stuck in your clothes or your own skin.

Kokyu-Dosa*

Kokyu-dosa is not wrestling. It is an exercise in mind extension and control of One-Point. With *nage* and *uke* in *seiza*

1. *Nage* extends arms, shoulder width apart. Palms are facing with fingers directed slightly up and elbows bent naturally.

2. *Uke* grasps *nage*'s wrists from the outside.

3. With Unbendable Arm and from One-Point, *nage* moves directly forward, unbalancing *uke*.

4. Hold down: Unbendable Arms with knife-edges of hands at *uke*'s shoulder and elbow.

If your practice deteriorates into a contest of weight and strength, please stop, center yourself and begin again, thinking not in terms of *what can I do against this opponent?* but *what can we do?*

What can *we* do? Well, *we* can go over *there* . . . .

Uke draws a circle to take you in. Draw yours larger. *Uke* drops One-Point. Drop yours lower. Ultimately, *kokyu-dosa* becomes an exercise in whose mind is larger, whose One-Point is lower. Having trouble? Think not of pushing *uke* over, but of giving *uke* and everything behind him a hug.

Faced with the challenge of kokyu-dosa with an armless student, it was decided to have uke put his fists at nage's shoulders. To succeed, nage had to mentally use uke's arms as his own and move with confidence. It worked very well with both uke and nage learning a valuable lesson. Now we practice this often with all students, for it provides valuable feedback on the power of mental intention and physical results.

— George Simcox

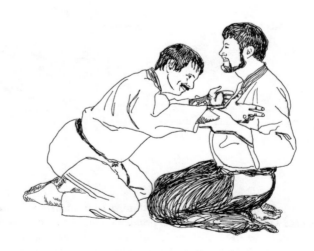

The mistake is to begin to think that budo means to have an opponent or an enemy; someone you want to be stronger than, someone you want to throw down. In true budo there is no enemy or opponent.

— *Morihei Ueshiba*

Leaning Backward*

An exercise in controlled relaxation and One-Point.

1. *Nage* leans back against *uke* but keeps One-Point.

2. *Uke* moves away suddenly.

    If *nage* has kept One-Point, stability will be maintained. If not, *nage* will fall.

Leaning Forward*

Another version of relaxing on a support while keeping One-Point.

1. *Nage* leans forward over *uke*.

2. *Uke* drops away suddenly.

   If *nage* has kept One-Point, stability will be maintained. If not, *nage* will fall.

   Note that arms are not kept artificially folded; they drop, relaxed, with *uke*, but body remains stable.

Raising Arms*

This can be thought of as a physical version of goal setting.

1. *Nage* bends backward with arms raised overhead but keeping One-Point.

2. *Uke* tests by pressing back at (perpendicular to) chest.

Notice that if arms are strongly extended, *nage* will be stable. If arms are extended weakly or hesitantly, stability will be lost.

One-Point With Attitude

As we have seen, attitude affects One-Point. But One-Point also affects attitude, or others' perception of it.

As demonstrated by Susan Chandler Sensei,

1. *Nage* purposely takes a position:

   a) Forward of One-Point,

   b) Over One-Point,

   c) Back of One-Point.

2. In each of these positions, *nage* recites a passage of poetry or the most matter-of-fact statement; strive for uniformity of intonation.

3. *Uke* observe:

   a) How the voice changes, despite *nage*'s best efforts at uniformity or subterfuge.

   b) The emotion conveyed or impact of the statement spoken in each of the three positions.

   c) With eyes closed, degree of success at guessing which position (forward of One-Point, over One-Point, or back of One-Point) *nage* is in at the moment.

Wrist Push*

This exercise appears on the *ki* test list as "Thrusting out one hand, then being pushed by the wrist" (*nage* stands in *hanmi*) and its variation, "Thrusting out one hand and raising one leg."

Both are an exercise in transferring energy to the One-Point. Doing so increases stability and flexibility at the same time. See "Floating-Foot Tenkan" on page 126.

Freedom From Fear

This is a classic yoga exercise. Watch for this pose in Eastern art and sculpture.

Nage stands with palms forward, the fingers of the left hand pointing up, fingers of the right hand pointing down.

Uke tests to the chest and back.

Are the results the same or different:

    a)   For right- and left-handed partners?

    b)   When the hand positions are reversed?

The Hum Test

In *seiza*,

1.   *Nage* hum a note. *Uke* test.

2.   *Nage* focus on the sound of a resonant bell. *Uke* test.

This is the auditory version of *tekubi-shindo undo* ("wrist shaking exercise"). See the last step in the Three-Minute *Ki* Exercise for Health (Appendix B).

Relax Completely

Relax Completely

Relaxation does not mean limpness or collapse. It means *not expending energy unnecessarily*, not diverting your energy to fighting yourself. A common example is that of a cat napping in a sunbeam. Her body is completely relaxed, yet if startled, she will be across the room in a flash.

Rigidity is not strength. If you try to make Unbendable Arm by making your arm rigid, you are actually hampering yourself and helping the opponent. Your stiff muscles make your arm harder for you to move, while making a wonderful lever for your opponent to move you.

A fundamental concept of Aikido is that just because an attacker controls your hand, he does not control the rest of you. The assumption in this equation is *relaxation*. When you are relaxed, the rest of you is free to move. When you are stiff and tense — the hand rigidly connected to a rigid arm, a tight body, tense legs, and a fixated mind — he *does* control the rest of you. It is the difference between pushing a broomstick across the floor and trying to push a rope across the floor.

Purely physical strength is limited by the physical body. There will always be someone bigger and stronger, if not now, then tomorrow or 20 years from now. O-Sensei was renowned for his strength and muscular build in his youth. By old age, when purely muscular strength may begin to fail, he had evolved beyond mere muscle and bone into other forms of strength.

Aikido allows you to use *uke*'s strength, instead of or in addition to your own, giving you a tremendous advantage over a larger, stronger opponent *provided you avoid a weight and strength contest*. Allowing the situation to deteriorate into a weight and strength contest throws away the advantage. In order to use *uke's* strength and energy, you must stay with it, align with it, go in the direction that it is going. Skillful blending with the attack is a form of camouflage, a weapon in and of itself.

As an example, suppose your Fairy Godmother has presented you with the Magic Cloak of Invisibility for a trip through the ogre's castle or the dragon's lair. What is the correct use of this weapon? It is to move softly and gently, leaving no trace of your passing.

To reveal your presence by stomping about, kicking over chairs, stopping to arm wrestle or punch out everyone you meet would be a waste of a powerful tool. By blending into the attacker's own power and direction you disappear; *uke* will feel only himself — not you — and be unable to counter.[8]

Acquiring this softness and sensitivity is one of the difficulties of Aikido. It is terribly tempting to attack *uke* with sheer muscle power if that is available to you; it is extremely difficult for the physically strong person to abandon what has always worked on weaker persons in favor of softness to all comers.

One of the strongest men I have ever known became thoroughly exasperated with my repeated attempts to muscle my way through a technique. "Time out!" he roared, dropped to the mat and challenged me to an arm wrestling match. Wham! He won. No contest. "Aha!" he said. "I *am* stronger than you. Just checking." Point taken.

Paradoxically, the more you feel that you have done nothing, the more likely it is that you have done the technique correctly. There is an enormous difference between attacking a technique and allowing a technique to happen and it is a difficult lesson to learn. One way out is to make softness itself a challenge. How softly and gently can you do a given technique? It is not necessary to slam and force the opponent.

A friend who saw Ueshiba doing a demonstration was impressed by the way this tiny, elderly man was laying the four or five big Air Force martial arts instructors down on the mat. What was most impressive was *how* he was doing it: "He almost *caressed* them down."

It is this softness and gentleness, this relaxation, that helps make Aikido so devastating, so irresistible, so effective.

---

[8] See *The Great Escape (Movies and Videos)*. Who escaped and why?

Relaxed Mind

Find and test someone engrossed in a conversation, a television show, a board game, or a book — test. Compare with someone who is not distracted; who has been warned and is therefore apprehensive about being "tested."

A classic response in *ki* class is known as the *Hakama* Effect, wherein a student does fine until a big, black *hakama* (the "skirt" worn by advanced students) looms before him. The student immediately thinks "Oh no! A test!" — and focusing on that, loses all stability.

For raw beginners, learning to roll safely is rarely the favorite exercise, especially if the student is focused on discomfort, fear, or embarrassment. A standard way around this, especially in children's classes, is Rolling Tag, played like any other game of tag except that players move only by rolling. It is astonishing how quickly rolls improve.

Relaxation and Rigidity

Tense arms or bodies make wonderful levers or targets for opponents. Relaxed ones do not.

Test the difference between lifting:

1. A 50-pound bag of rice and

2. A 50-pound rod or weight bar.

Repeat with relaxed body and a purposely rigid body. See also "Unliftable Body" on page 92.

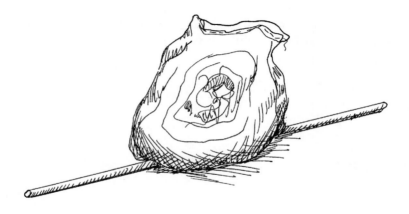

Tense attitudes are also detrimental to those who hold them and their situations in life. Sensei Dan Frank of the Maryland Ki Society tells of a policeman with a long history of persons resisting arrest. He studied Aikido in order to learn to apply effective wrist locks, but first had to learn how to relax and be centered. He did so — only to discover that he no longer needed wrist locks and control techniques. Because he was approaching situations relaxed, rather than with a belligerent mind or the expectation of conflict, he had no more problems with persons resisting arrest.

"No pain, No gain"

In many traditional *dojos*, stretching is done in pairs who may "help" each other by standing on knees or back — then wonder why the former partner doesn't return.

Ki classes encourage limbering, but not extreme muscle tension.

Here's why.

Doing toe-touching or other stretching exercises in pairs,

1. *Nage* forces a stretch while thinking of the old saw "no pain, no gain." *Uke* test.

2. *Nage* moves forward just until the muscle reaches its comfortable limit. *Uke* test.

Arm Swinging*

In class, this exercise (*ude-furi undo*) is usually continuous with the Spinning Exercise (*ude-furi choyaku undo*).

Nage stands with feet shoulder-width apart, with head, eyes, and chest straight ahead. *Uke* calls the count.

1. On "One," swing arms to the left, wrapping around body.

2. On "Two," swing arms to the right, wrapping around body.

   The count is 1-2, 1-2, 1-2, 1-2 . . . until *uke* or the instructor signals the end of the series by calling a 3 - 4.

3. On "Three," swing arms to left as on "One."

4. On "Four," swing arms right as you step forward with left foot.

Uke may test for stability at this point, or *nage* may continue into the Spinning Exercise (*Ude-furi Choyaku Undo*) on count of "One".

Spinning*

An exercise (*ude-furi choyaku undo*) to develop balance, One-Point, and relaxation. Remember spinning like a top when you were a child? Movement begins from the One-Point, although rapid changes in direction can start from the little finger which acts like a small starter motor. Arms are not *held* out, they *spin* out due to centrifugal force; they should be so relaxed that you can feel tingling in the fingers. Extend *ki*, that is, have a goal. Pick a point on two walls to serve as reference points, otherwise you will become dizzy and disoriented.

From Step 4 of the Arm Swinging Exercise, with arms wrapped to right side of body and left foot forward,

1. On "One," rotate One-Point 180 degrees. Arms spin out rising to shoulder height, then wrapping to left side of body.

2. On "Two," reverse direction returning to original position with arms wrapped to right side of body.

   The count is 1-2, 1-2, 1-2, 1-2 . . . until uke or the instructor signals the end of the series by calling a 3 - 4.

Bowing*

From *seiza,*

1. *Nage* bows forward from the One-Point by sliding hands from the thighs to the mat to form a triangle. Forehead is a few inches above the hands, parallel to the floor. Eyes follow direction of head.

2. *Nage* holds this position for three seconds, then rises.

3. *Uke* tests by:

   a) Pushing *nage* from side while bowing down and while coming up.

   b) Standing behind, holding *nage's* shoulders to prevent bow.

In karate, opponents keep eyes warily on each other during the bow. In Aikido partners lower the eyes with the head in an act of mutual respect and trust. Saotome (1993) explains why.

Reigi is often translated as "courtesy" or "etiquette" but the meaning is much richer. Rei ... translates as "Holy Spirit"; gi is "manifestation." Bowing to another is the recognition of this responsibility and of the spirit of [God] within each person.

— Mitsugi Saotome

A *nage* adept at controlling relaxation, rigidity, and balance can put on quite a show:

1. Sliding sideways across the mat, then

2. Relaxing and dropping weight underside.

    For *uke*, the feeling is like hitting a soft, thick, and utterly unmovable rubber wall.

In a more martial version of the bow, the left hand is placed on the mat, followed by the right (sword hand).

The Virginia Ki Society specifically uses the version described here (also used in Zen Buddhism).

— George Simcox

The Nelsons

In pairs, with *uke* standing behind *nage* of approximately equal height, *uke* slips arms under *nage's* arms, then up, clasping hands behind *nage's* neck to bend neck and body forward.

This is the wrestling hold known as the Full Nelson. (One hand holding behind the neck is a Half Nelson).

Experiment with these situations:

    a)   *Nage* tenses and stiffens. Observe results.

    b)   *Nage* relaxes, drops One-Point, arms, and shoulders. Observe results. (Compare "Unliftable Body.")

    c)   *Nage* stays relaxed throughout.

If some guy wants to come out of a dark alley and grab you around the neck, that is <u>his</u> problem. If you are so frightened and paralyzed that you are unable to act, that is <u>your</u> problem.

—George Simcox

"Strong" and "Soft"

Nage presents a fist or fists tightly balled with muscles "strongly" tensed. *Uke* takes *nage*'s wrist and provides motion such as:

    a)   Pushing and pulling,

    b)   Turning wrists in and out,

    c)   Extending down and pulling up.

Uke asks *nage* to identify the motion then have *nage* relax arm.

Nage will feel only the strongest motions while tense. If for example, *uke* is rotating *nage*'s wrists in, *nage* may not have a clue as to what is happening. On relaxing, however, the wrists will actually turn in, a motion that was there all along but imperceptible to rigid muscles.

Uke should make these motions increasingly subtle as *nage* improves in the ability to feel them while relaxed. This exercise can flow into "Sticky Hands."

As we progress we learn to be softer. It is the young karate students who do the smashing blocks. The Old Master has learned to do just enough to deflect a blow, to brush it softly aside. In Aikido, softness is taught from the beginning.

— *D. C. Buchanan*

Sticky Hands

An exercise in feeling. *Uke* and *nage* touch hands or fingers, as:

1. *Uke* moves hands slowly and smoothly about.

2. *Nage* follows *uke*'s motions without breaking contact, accepting a push, following a pull. As skill develops,

    a) *Uke* tries to touch *nage* gently on the nose or chest.

    b) *With hands apart, nage*, with eyes closed, follows *uke*'s movements by sensing the heat of *uke*'s hands.

Move slowly at first and avoid shoving or yanking contests. Speed is not the real purpose, nor is touching the nose. As in most Aikido techniques, contact with uke is not to grab, crush, or block but to feel or sense position. Many people with bad eyes have ended up in Aikido rather than other martial arts because if all you can see is a blur you must rely on feeling. Those with good eyes can overcome their handicap of good vision by closing eyes or practicing in a dimly lit room.

The Linebacker Versus the Water Drop

With *uke* in a braced standing position,

1. *Nage* pushes directly into *uke* with strength. *Uke* will probably be very stable.

2. *Nage* pushes softly into *uke*. This time *nage* should be able to feel the points of weakness and move with them.

Also try this exercise:

a) In the karate wide-stance position.

b) In *hanmi.*

In this and the "Stiff Fist" exercise, relaxing allows nage to feel and follow the little areas of weakness or instability, like a tiny drop of water trickling through a small hole, along any available channel, in a way that a brick or a boulder could never do.

Stiff Fist

Uke extends a strong stiff arm with a stiff fist.

1. *Nage* squeezing firmly, tries to move it in different directions.
2. *Nage* surrounds it lightly and moves it softly.

What *Doesn't* He Have?

In pairs or in groups of three,

1. *Uke* seizes *nage*'s wrist. Leaving wrist in place,

2. *Nage* takes inventory of what *uke* does *not* control.

For example, the *uke* who seizes *nage's* shoulder does not control *nage's* other shoulder.

The *uke* who seizes *nage's* hand does not control *nage's* hips, foot, other hand, or shoulders.

Compare with "Letting Go" (page 81) an exercise in which you will consider that *uke* does not control your elbow.

During a drug enforcement training program, one participant, a former Golden Gloves champion, had a pistol in one hand. His instructor pinned that hand to the wall. At any point, this champion boxer could have pounded him with his free hand, but did not. Because all his attention was concentrated on trying to make that pistol work, his mind was closed to all the other tools and options at his command.

— George Simcox

Letting Go

Every child is told the story of the Monkey Trap, a box with a hole and nuts or fruit inside. A monkey can reach through the hole to the goodies inside, but cannot withdraw the full, clenched fist. We often understand this tale as a parable or laugh at the foolishness of these "lower" creatures when, in fact, it describes a standard *human* response. Here *uke's* fingers form the opening and *nage's* fist is a fist, whether it holds nuts — or thin air.

1. *Uke* holds *nage*'s wrist in a firm grasp. *Nage* attempts to pull away but will be stopped by his own fist.

2. *Nage* relaxes, imagines hand shrinking smaller and smaller, then, extending *ki* from fingers and elbow, pulls away.

Uke and *nage* compare effort and success of pulling away.

Often when we think we are pulling away we aren't — we're actually holding on.

In the first case, the two are held tightly together by *nage's* own rigid fist which gives *uke* something to hold on to.

In the second case, *uke* simply goes away. Completely.

Please note that this is a *ki* exercise, not an exercise in "breaking a hold." We rarely break holds or grabs — because in Aikido a hold is an *advantage*.

Keeping the hold means *uke* has just committed (tied up) up at least one of his weapons. The hold tells *nage* exactly where *uke* is, and presents *nage* with a gift of energy while limiting *uke's* options.

Breaking the hold means starting over at the point where *uke* has not committed to any particular attack and so has all options open. *Nage* doesn't know where *uke* is, and has no physical energy or inertia to work with.

Keep Weight Underside

Keep Weight Underside

Aikido does not fight the force of gravity — it takes advantage of it. *Weight underside* is the most efficient approach to a motion as it aligns with the forces of nature, the forces of the universe.

Those forces are more powerful than we usually realize. Drop your hand and gravity alone will move it towards the center of the earth at the rate of 32 feet per second squared. And the expression:

$$F = ma$$

(Force = mass X acceleration)

is the fundamental law of physics behind the ancient observation that "the bigger they are, the harder they fall."

A full-sized sheet of newspaper spread out flat on a table top has 10,000 pounds of air pressing on its surface. Don't believe it? Slide a wooden yardstick under a sheet of newspaper; strike down sharply on the protruding end of the yardstick and see what happens.

Most Aikido techniques will not work with the shoulders up and elbows held out to the side. But why waste energy holding shoulders and elbows against the force of gravity and weight of air? Align with those forces; drop them.

Under stress, we tend to hunch our bodies as if protecting ourselves against an attacker. Shoulders go up and elbows go out, perhaps a

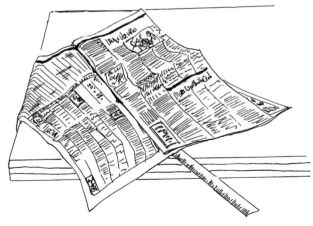

primeval device to look bigger than we are. In reality, a hunched body is no protection at all. Relax. Check periodically for signs of tension. Is your face tight? Relax your eyelids. Are your shoulders hunched while driving or working at your desk? Drop them.

We may also be disturbed by hunched attitudes — defense mechanisms, often brilliant survival techniques — that served their purpose years ago but are no longer useful, may actually be harmful, and so are no protection either. "He's *very* defensive," said an observant friend of a fiercely tough-guy acquaintance, "*and so he is very easily manipulated.*"

For me, another version of Weight Underside came to light with an injury. As there always seems to be more to do than can possibly be done, I tend to flit from one crisis to another, lopping the heads off the dandelions of life rather then reaching down to the root.

When flitting meant hobbling painfully about on a severely sprained ankle or on crutches, I was astonished to find that I accomplished *more*. I had to stay in one place, finish what I had begun, and follow the chore through to the end instead of making do with "a lick and a promise."

To my surprise, this did not mean lost time but a product: a series of completed tasks in place of divided attention, wasted energies, and an endless stream of unfinished work and emotional IOUs.

Arm Dropping*

This seemingly simple exercise (*udemawashi-undo*) is the basis of many Aikido throws. It produces the "up" that makes an effective "down." It is an exercise in raising the arm and dropping it in alignment with gravity, using relaxation, mass and acceleration in the most effective way possible.

Standing with feet shoulder-width apart, *nage* will:

1.   Raise arm to the highest point possible without straightening, stiffening or locking the elbow.

2.   *Allow* the arm to drop, of its own weight, to the lowest point.

3.   *Uke* test by attempting to lift straight up on the arm or testing for Unbendbable Arm.

The same approach underlies sword techniques and other tools from hammers to hoes. These fall of their own weight. They are not forced up then forced down. To do so is tiring and inefficient. Variation: Some Aikido techniques require ducking a strike. Which is quicker? Dropping the body? or lifting the feet?

The Light Pole

In *seiza*,

1. *Nage* imagines a shaft of light, like a fireman's pole, up through the top of the head, extending down through One-Point, and out through the ends of the universe.

2. *Nage* imagines sliding gently down that shaft of light or riding an elevator down towards the center of the earth and beyond. *Uke* test.

Dinosaurs and Sand

For imaginary size and weight, be a dinosaur with a 40-foot tail.

Consider an hourglass and watch the grains of sand falling down.

1. Imagine that you are the hourglass, warm sand running through the top of your head, streaming through your body.

2. Change the sand grains into individual grains of light.

3. Imagine what light would look like if it were a liquid. Send this warm honey-colored liquid through your body, to drain out through holes in your hands and feet. *Uke* test.

Unraisable Arm*

An exercise in *doing* nothing.

1. *Nage* lays arm in *uke*'s hands and imagines it heavy — full of lead shot, or with fingers hooked under a fence wire.

2. *Uke* gently removes supporting hands.

3. *Uke* test by lifting up gently behind the elbow.

    Nage does nothing, changes nothing. If *uke* wants to lift the arm, he must be allowed to lift all of it — all by himself.

"Do nothing! Doing nothing" is not the same as "not doing anything."

— *Koichi Tohei*

Think of buoyancy rather than weight and float your arms in a swimming pool. Close your eyes, experience the feeling, then recreate it in air. Visit an aquarium that has seabirds and an underwater view at feeding time. Watch the birds diving, wheeling, soaring — flying through the water. To them there is no difference between the fluid air and the fluid water.

Unliftable Hand*

With *nage* in *seiza*,

1. *Uke* attempts to lift *nage*'s hand as it rests on the thigh.

    The test is up along the arm towards the shoulder (not straight up from the knee).

Uke may choose to see this as an attempt to lift nage's hand. Nage can choose to see this as Unbendable Arm or as uke's attempt to lift the attached leg and entire body by the one hand — in the sense of "If you're going to move me, you're going to have to move all of me" — obviously an impossible task.

Unliftable Body*

In groups of three,

1. Tension — Two *ukes* lift *nage* by grasping *nage's* upper arms. *Nage* keeps arms and body rigid.

2. Relaxation — *Nage* keeps arms vertical but relaxed, shoulders down, while imagining extending to the center of the earth.

3. Compare with tense arms and raised shoulders.

During the formal *ki* test, the instructor attempts to lift *nage* from the front. In practice, inexperienced *ukes* bend and tilt and push, striving for maximum mechanical advantage — skewing the test. Eliminate this by having two *ukes* lifting by *nage's* arms as shown.

Nage's arms must be straight. It is possible for *nage* to "pass" this test through basic physics by simply moving the elbows slightly forward of the body — but that is not the *ki* exercise.

To be really sporting, test with *nage* sitting in a chair. Lift chair.

Floating Below

Because these exercises are done with the mind, you can do anything, unlimited by the constraints of the physical world. For example, if the instructor tells you to "float," why limit yourself to floating above the mat?

a) *Float under* the mat or underground with just your eyes peeking up above the mat or above the grass.

b) Sit at the bottom of a quarry, at the bottom of the sea, at the very center of the earth.

c) Float in a bubble in Outer Space where there is no up or down.

d) Be a leaf floating downstream with the current.

Uke test at *nage's* request.

Extend Ki

Extend Ki

If *ki* is defined as "mind" or "attention" then "extending *ki*" refers to a directing of mind or attention to a thing, to a point of focus, to a goal. The phrase "extend *ki*" seems to suggest that there is a starting point, a time when *ki* is *not* being extended. Actually *ki* should be extended all the time. In Aikido and in daily life, waiting until an attack occurs, and then trying to extend, attend, or set a goal, is too late. Hence a slightly different translation:

"Ki is extending."

Why do you have to "extend *ki*"? Well, you don't. You can also think of your body filled with light. But the concept of something going out of your body is easier to grasp. The next step, learning to align with the extension of energy from your partner and dealing with it appropriately, is the beginning of Aikido technique.

There is sometimes discussion of the power of mechanics versus *ki*. Actually there is no "versus" — the two work in harmony. *Ki* helps the mechanics to work more effectively while proper mechanics allow the *ki* to flow. We all extend *ki* ("mind" or "attention") when driving a car or riding a bicycle. The task would be dangerously difficult if we limited attention to the few inches of road just beneath the tires. (Remember trying to align the hood ornament with the side of the road when learning to drive?)

How well you "drive" an Aikido technique depends on where you place your mind. If you do not extend *ki* during a technique or while under attack, you will tend to let your mind stop at the hand (just as you programmed your partner's mind to stop at a green light (see *Introduction*). A *nage* who cuts a technique short tends to push into *uke*'s power, ending up in a strength and weight contest. A *nage* who leads the mind outside *uke*'s power can drop *uke* to the mat with seemingly impossible, magical ease.

Extending *ki* involves not only extending your own *ki*, but perceiving it as extended in others and aligning with that flow, that energy, that attention. You do not extend *ki* at the same instant that you step onto a moving escalator. You first find one that is going the way you want to go, align with it, evaluating and matching speed and direction, then go on your way.

Tenkan ("turning") appears to be a physical technique, but it is based on internal attitude and direction, blending and flow. It can also be done verbally and emotionally — and must be practiced in these ways to be truly understood.

I once worked in a technical reports unit responsible for turning the engineers' reports into meaningful English. A certain engineer had a reputation of being hard to deal with, difficult, cantankerous, and sometimes downright abusive; he had even threatened to kick one arrogant young editor down the stairs if he ever touched his stuff again. There was simply no working with him, went the report, and as the New Kid on the Block, the next sacrificial lamb, I was sent down to "try to deal with him."

He glared ferociously as I walked in. As this did not seem to be the time to launch into a lecture on technical style, I asked him instead to tell me about his project.

And he did, with enthusiasm and passion. He made the circuits and wires and pins and the rationale behind the design *fascinating*.

"And right now," I said, "this report does not do your work justice." He blinked. "Oh," he said. "*Can you please help me?*"

Because I meant what I said and because there was no "technique" involved I didn't understand quite what had happened. Nor did I quite understand why this supposedly fierce and ferocious man turned out to be a gracious, courtly, and delightful gentleman.

Now I have a name for it. Blending, seeing things from the other person's point of view, *tenkan*.

Water Pump

This is a basic image for visualizing flow of *ki*.

1. *Nage* imagines a water pump at One-Point, with water whooshing up from the cosmos, through the One-Point and out through the water hose (arm). Draw lines on the opposite wall with a finger.

2. *Uke* test for Unbendable Arm.

Unbendable Arm*

For a basic discussion of Unbendable Arm, refer to "Unbendable Arm" on page 18 of the *Introduction*.

Also experiment with the following variations.

a) Extend arm tense, tight, "strong." Observe effort required by *nage* to bend it; on *uke* to keep it straight.

b) Extend arm tense and tight, then relax into Unbendable Arm.

c) Unbendable Arm in any position from straight to bent.

d) Unbendable Arm with the fingers bent up.

Here *nage* must think of extending *ki* out the wrist rather than the fingertips. (*Uke* bend fingers *gently*!)

Once Unbendable Arm has been mastered it becomes easy to keep an Unbendable Arm separate from the rest of the body. In *Shin-Shin Toitsu Aikido* we look not only for "mind-body" coordination but also for "body-body" coordination. Coordination between arm and body does not necessarily exist if *nage* thinks only of sending a stream of *ki* out the arm. *Uke* can detect this disassociation easily: instead of trying to bend the arm, *lift* the arm — "Unbendable Body."

Nage, instead of concentrating on sending *ki* through the arm only, must imagine *ki* streaming out from the One-Point, an expanding bubble of *ki* that *includes* the arm — but is not limited to it.

See also the comments under testing for "Unliftable Hand" (page 91). Note the idea that if *uke* is going to lift the hand he will have to lift the entire body.

In psychology, Unbendable Arm is considered a sign of deep hypnosis; the patient is convinced by the practitioner that the arm is unbendable.

In Aikido the arm may be unbendable but is under the control of the Aikidoist, not someone else.

Walking with Unbendable Arm*

Walking with Unbendable Arm can change *nage's* point of view from simply trying to pass the test to providing a definite goal towards which *ki* or attention can be extended.

1. *Nage* makes an Unbendable Arm,

2. *Nage* walks forward.

3. *Uke*, standing to the side, attempts to halt *nage* by pushing against the chest (not an arm across the throat, please).

If *nage* extends *ki* — *attention, purpose, and goal* — out beyond *uke*'s focus, *uke* will be unable to stop the motion. If *uke* has fixed attention and energy on *nage's* arm, no energy is left over to resist forward movement and *uke* is irresistibly drawn along with *nage*.

Always give the attacker what he wants, with a little bit more. Does uke want the hand? Then give him the hand; that is his battlefield. Let him have his battlefield — now you move the earth.

— *George Simcox*

Shaking Hands

What is it that is so different between a limp handshake, a firm one, and a "hand buster"?

In groups of four,

1. Two *nages* shake hands.

2. Two *ukes* test for Unbendable Arm.

a) Alternate *nages* extend *ki*.

b) Both *nages* extend *ki*.

c) Each *nage* extend appreciation and joy to the other.

d) Each *nage* imagine wanting to be elsewhere.

Ki Door

This exercise combines *ki* with mechanics. If a door is not available, it can also be done with *uke* standing with an arm extended.

1. Try to push your way through a heavy door while placing your mind behind you or *not* extending.

2. Compare with the feel of walking through the door while directing your mind forward and extending.

3. Repeat while extending as above — but this time push the door open *from the hinge side*.

The OK Test

An example of *ki* flow coupled with the mechanics of anatomy.

1. *Nage* touches thumb and forefinger and tries to hold the two fingers together while *uke* attempts to pull them apart.

2. *Nage* imagines *ki* flowing in a ring around the joined fingers. *Uke* test. *Nage* concentrates on One-Point. *Uke* test.

3. *Nage* bends the wrist at 90 degrees. *Uke* compare the forces necessary to pull the fingers apart. *Nage* compare the amount of effort required to keep them together.

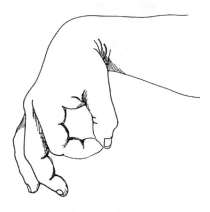

The 90-degree wrist bend is the proper position for various Aikido wristlocks. This exercise reveals part of the reason for the importance and effectiveness of the 90-degree bend. Ki flows best in association with proper mechanics.

It also flows best where there is no internal dissonance. For students with upcoming school exams ("How do you like your English class?" or "How are you doing in Math?") uke (or Mom and Dad) can tell just by testing.

Rolling With a Goal

Working in groups of three,

1. *Nage* rolls forward and back (*koho-tento-undo*). *Uke* tests by standing *behind nage* and pulling back from shoulders. If *nage*'s mind is on the test and the tester, *nage* will topple backwards.

2. With *uke* in the same position and offering the same test, have *nage* explain the process to a third partner sitting several feet away and facing *nage*. *Uke* test while *nage* is extending his mind in explaining the exercise.

Steven R. Covey, author of the highly successful series "The Seven Habits of Highly Successful People," insists that it is not enough to simply study the habits — you must teach them to another. Changing role from student to teacher changes you.

What you learn today, you can teach another tomorrow. If you know one thing, teach one thing.

— Koichi Tohei

Block Hands

In karate, the breaking of bricks and blocks with bare hands is taught not only as a weapon, but to develop concentration, focus, and mind control. If the mind stops at the target, the hand stops at the target. If the mind continues through, the hand continues through. This exercise demonstrates the same internal focus and results.

1. *Uke* presents hands as shown, heels of hands firmly together (fingers and thumbs well apart for safety).

2. *Nage* strikes down (*shomen-uchi*) to center of hands while:

    a) Focusing on the hands as target.

    b) Focusing and extending *past* the hands.

    Observe *nage*'s success in "breaking the block" depending on point of focus.

Shomen-uchi ("front strike") is done as follows. In left *hanmi*, raise extended right arm straight up overhead. Strike straight down while stepping forward into right *hanmi*.

Sankyo*

As Aikido technique, *sankyo* involves rotating the arm and wrist toward the body. It serves as a wrist-lock and come-along.

As *ki* exercise, the wrist is *not* twisted. If it is, the arms follow the upward motion of the wrist; the slightest upward push under *nage's* wrist will easily raise *nage's* arms.

1. *Nage* assumes *sankyo.*

2. *Uke* tests by pressing into *nage's* hands (towards chest).

3. *Nage* experiment with the following. *Uke* test by pushing into hands and by attempting to lift *nage's* arms:

   a) Extending arms out from body.

   b) Pulling arms close into chest.

   c) Rotating wrist. (Rotation is along axis of arm so that thumb goes away from *nage,* and then up.)

Go with the Flow — Sankyo

A test for the claim that Mind leads Body.

In pairs,

1. *Nage* assumes *sankyo* (see page 108) and imagines *ki* flowing in a circle around the arms, clockwise or counterclockwise.

2. *Uke* test by pressing the elbow from the side and trying to guess in which direction *nage* is driving his "*ki* circuit." (It will be easier to move the elbow in the direction of flow.)

3. *Nage* vary these two possibilities with a third: *ki* expanding from One-Point outward in all directions. *Uke* test.

Go With the Flow — Jo Exercise

In groups of three, with a *jo* (staff or a broomstick),

1. Two *ukes* pull on opposite ends.

2. *Nage* in middle pushes stick in one direction or the other.

   Observe the little effort required to move the *jo* or an *uke* by joining with the other. Does this change with attempt to move the *jo* rather than the *uke*?

   Observe effort required if *nage* thinks of joining *uke 1* and:

   a) *Opposing* the actions of *uke 2.*

   b) *Helping uke 1* do what he is already doing.

Go With the Flow — Mini-Jo

Instead of *jo* and three partners, the exercise on page 110 can be done with two partners — and a pencil.

1. *Uke* pulls on the two ends of the pencil.

2. *Nage* pushes in one direction or the other.

As in the previous exercises, *nage* observes the effort required if thinking of:

a) *Pushing* against one hand, *or*

b) *Helping the other hand* do what it is already doing.

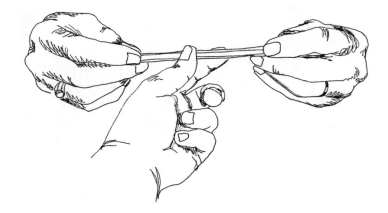

St. Jerome, when granted his request to see Heaven and Hell, was surprised to see in Hell a great dinner party. In a great hall of infinite length was an infinitely long table, loaded with every delight known to a hungry person — but the people were starving and desperate. Every hand ended in a fork ten feet long and because they could not get the food into their own mouths, all were frantically trying to snatch food from one other.

Heaven. Same hall, same table, same ten-foot forks, but the people were smiling, happy, and having a wonderful time, for instead of each one desperately trying to feed himself, they were feeding each other.

Teamwork works better.

Go With the Flow — Arm Pulling

In groups of three, do the same exercise as with the *jo,* but,

1. Two *ukes* pull on *nage*'s arms.

2. *Nage* relaxes, extends *ki*, joining with one or the other and moving in that direction.

   What is the difference between:

   a) Pushing against one *uke*, and

   b) Helping the other *uke* pull?

Go With the Flow — Pushups

Aikido rarely blocks, never stops, does not jerk or pause, but continues and transforms motion. This continuity seems difficult to learn, but nearly everyone used it regularly — to survive gym class.

1. Do 10-20 pushups. Note the amount of effort required.

2. Rest.

3. Do a second set of 10-20 pushups, but do them as follows:

    a) Lie facedown on mat, palms up on back.

    b) Place hands on mat; do one pushup.

    c) Return to position a) and repeat.

        This procedure eliminates motion, inertia, and all possibility of following and flowing with the upward or downard motion.

        Note the number of pushups done, and the effort required to do them.

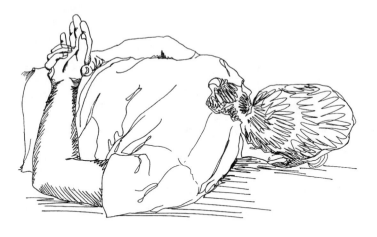

This is the difference between following *the flow of energy and inertia in a technique and trying to* force *a technique under your own power.*

Additive Ki

Ki can be added, joined, and extended from one person to another. In groups of three,

1. *Uke 1* test *nage* with Unbendable Arm, *seiza*, or any other test to determine the point of failure.

2. *Uke 2*, in position behind *nage* (out of sight), lightly touch *nage* and extend *ki* out to *uke* 1.

3. *Uke 1* test *nage* with the same amount of effort as required previously to reach failure.

Variations:

a) Do the same test but absorb *ki.*

b) Have a fourth partner test *uke* 2.

In the Greek New Testament, the word most commonly used for prayer was prosechein, a vow, a declaration, a promise of action, a directing of attention to a thing, far different from the medieval image of the helpless, humble supplicant. Now, the idea of joining with God, playing on his team, is a radical, even shocking approach to prayer. But here is the ancient, underlying rationale.

Sending Ki

In groups of two or three or more as *nage*, each with an *uke*,

1. Each *uke* test *nage* for "baseline" stability.

2. All *nages* extend *ki* to one nage. *Uke* test.

Variations:

a) Does the intention of those extending *ki* matter? What if their image is to bowl one *nage* over?

b) What happens if positive or negative *ki* is extended around the circle (from one to another in sequence rather than all extending to one *nage*)?

Bouncing Ki

In groups of two or three,

1. *Nage* places a hand on floor; *uke* presses and extends *ki* down on *nage*'s hand. *Nage* tries to lift the hand with muscle. Note effort required.

2. *Nage* imagines joining with *uke*'s downward *ki* and sending it all down to the center of the earth; it bounces back to help lift the hand.

Compare the effort involved with "bouncing *ki*" to the effort required to lift the hand through sheer muscle and determination.

Work with one *uke* pressing one hand, or two *uke*s, one for each hand. (During the technique, the second *uke* may test *nage* for stability.)

Absorbtion and Extension

Ki can be extended *or* absorbed.

1. *Uke* places a hand on *nage's* chest or hand, palm to palm.

2. *Nage* imagines receiving and absorbing *uke*'s *ki*.

3. *Nage* or a third partner presses down on *uke*'s wrist. Notice the amount of effort needed to brush the hand away.

4. *Nage* imagines *ki* streaming out in all directions from One-Point, like an expanding bubble of light.

5. *Uke* or a third partner presses down on *uke*'s wrist. Notice the amount of effort needed to brush the hand away.

Around 1941, Life Magazine ran a photo of wrestler Dick ("The Bruiser") Addis attempting to lift a small man who placed his finger gently under the big man's chin. Addis could not lift him. The suggestion was made that the finger made a connection so that Addis was forced to lift his own weight along with that of the other person.

We would say that it was just ki transfer and could have involved any finger to any part of the body. But, then again, who would believe such "nonsense" when the other explanation is so "logical"?

— *George Simcox*

a) Repeat using the "Yes and No" test (page 129).

b) Repeat these steps using dark thoughts, happy thoughts or other images. (See *Meditation*.)

c) Apply to *tenkan*, an exercise which alternates absorbtion and extension.

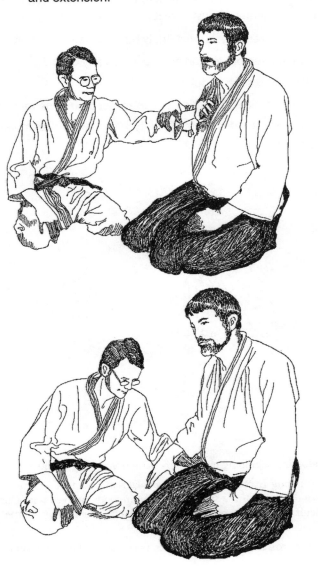

Disrupting Mind — Wrist Tickle

Part of Aikido technique is causing *uke* to *want* to move. (Or, in the vernacular, "messing with his mind.") When *uke* holds with firm but neutral energy it is difficult to do *tenkan* as there is nothing to work with. With no flow, there is nowhere to go. But *nage* can change the equation with a tiny, almost invisible motion that draws *uke's* mind.

1. *Uke* seizes *nage's* wrist firmly but with neutral energy.

2. *Nage* attempts *tenkan* and observes any difficulty.

3. Return to starting point.

4. *Nage* strokes underside of *uke's* wrist then turns *tenkan*.

5. Observe the degree of difficulty in the two *tenkan* motions.

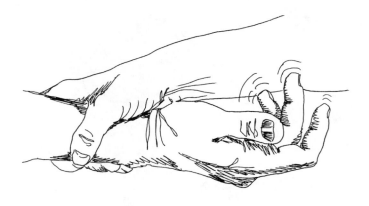

In Aikido, tiny beginning motions are behind many big results.

In the Spinning Exercise (*ude-furi choyaku undo* on page 71), turning and changing direction of the spin with the entire body or even with One-Point is difficult. Begin the motion with a finger that acts like a little starter motor.

A backward roll begins not by flinging back the head but by a subtle tilt of the pelvis.

Mind Leading Body

In many warm-up exercises, such as the "Three-Minute *Ki* Exercise for Health" (Appendix B), movements are performed two or more times on a side.

1. *Nage* do an exercise such as Arm-Swinging Exercise twice on a side; *uke* test.

2. *Nage* do the exercise once on each side; *uke* test.

3. Repeat the sequence, but this time for Step 2 ("once on each side"), first imagine doing the movement, then follow with the physical motion. *Uke* test.

Notice the sensations of your body during the exercise. Practice recreating the sensations and imaging the motion in your mind. In this way, the mind forms a "template" for the upcoming physical action.

Just Do It

With *uke* holding *nage*'s palm-down wrist (*katate-tori*),

1. *Nage* determines the energy and force needed to pull away (or if pulling away is even possible). Returning to starting position, this time,

2. *Nage* looks at fingernails, reaches reach up and adjusts glasses or pats the hair.

3. Compare the energy necessary to perform these familiar motions to the energy needed to *pull* away from the hold.

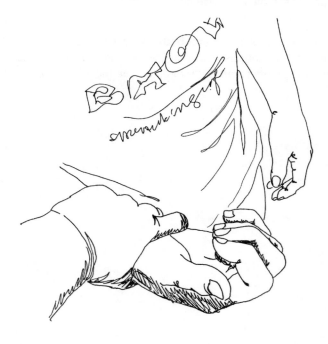

Women are said to typically "look at their fingernails" with the hand palm down, men with the palm up. For this exercise, start with palm down then rotate hand palm up to look at nails. This rotation of the hand, like other rotational movements, is extremely difficult to stop.

Tenkan on a String

In *tenkan* techniques it is extremely common for beginners to back up rather than to move forward.

A *nage* extending *ki* and moving *forward* is the center of the circle. *Uke*, rotating around the outside, is at a disadvantage.

Moving *backward* makes *uke* the center of the circle and puts *nage*, rotating around *uke*, at the disadvantage.

1. Make the actual motion and *ki* extension visible with a rag, a washcloth, a belt, or a string.

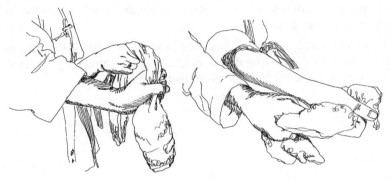

Backing up looks like this.   Extending looks like this.

(Nage's hand is inside.   Uke's hand is outside.)

2. *Uke* and *nage* trade places. *Uke* notice how the *tenkan* feels when *nage* moves forward; when *nage* moves back. Which is more compelling?

Tenkan absorbs and redirects *oncoming* energy. If *uke* pulls back, experienced *nages* switch to an entering technique (*irimi*) because *tenkan* won't work. *Uke* must *extend* forward rather than requiring *nage* to *drag* him forward. For an exercise in learning the proper feeling, see "Rag-Doll Tenkan" on page 127.

Aikido has been described as The Art of Leading. It is also The Art of Following as one must follow and align before one can effectively lead.

— Susan Chandler

Balloon Tenkan

Because *ki* tends to flow in the direction that the fingers are pointing, the first step in *tenkan* is to curl the fingers (see page 34) in order to blend with and redirect *uke*'s *ki*. A big strong *nage* may be able to muscle and force the issue with a small *uke*, but this approach can't win against a *balloon*. *Nage* must curve the fingers, must concentrate on extending *ki* and blending, or else the balloon will go wafting, skipping and dancing across the room.

No fair holding it with two hands except at beginning and end. Also, keep fingers together and curved — this is not an exercise in *gripping* the balloon with big basketball hands. It is an exercise in *controlling* the balloon.

This technique is similar to that used in lacrosse. The ball is kept in the basket by controlling direction and inertia. Think of your hand as the basket and the balloon as the ball.

Floating-Foot Tenkan

When doing a *tenkan*, *nage* commonly slides forward with the same-side (forward) foot, then turns. With anything less than a cooperative *uke*, there is the possibility of collision.

Instead of sliding directly forward, *nage* will,

1. Lift the front foot, then

2. Enter and turn 180 degrees (as for any *tenkan*).

The momentary balancing on one foot makes *nage,* like the balloon, sensitive to the slightest force or energy from *uke*. *Nage* naturally goes around and collision is avoided.

Starting and ending attacks, techniques, and rolls on one foot develops balance, timing, and a greater awareness of the energy involved. (It also protects against the dreaded "*Hakama* Toe," toes tangled in the folds of the skirt worn by advanced students.)

"Turn the other cheek," said Jesus, in a call for restraint and patience. It is a challenge to be more than an automatic stimulus-response machine programmed to explode into rage or revenge at any perceived affront or insult. This exercise in pacifism ("peacefulness") and self-control has been misunderstood by many to mean an exercise in passivism and masochism.

Much of the confusion over the morality of pacifism versus "violence" is due to a faulty understanding of good and evil. This begins with the misperception that goodness is inactive and dull, while evil is active and interesting. When Good is limited to passive stonewalling in the face of active, aggressive Evil, the exercise becomes: "Can I continue turning the other cheek long enough that he wears out his arm hitting me, gets bored, and goes away?" This protects neither the attacked, the attacker, nor the overall situation.

"'Turn the other cheek' is Aiki," said Ueshiba. "But in Aikido, we would turn before the blow. Thus the attacked is saved from pain and the attacker is saved from sin."

Rag-Doll Tenkan

In Aikido *tenkan* techniques, the competitive or hesitant *uke* (who knows what's coming) may pull back. The inexperienced *nage* may valiantly attempt to drag the unwilling *uke* around in a circle.

This exercise allows *uke* to practice extending forward while *nage* practices accepting and aligning with the energy. In pairs,

1. *Nage* extends a wrist and stands with One-Point.

2. *Uke* takes the wrist and pushes *nage* around in a circle.

   A strange feeling? This is how it *should* feel.

When true serenity is gained,
To bow and to bend we will not be ashamed.
To turn and to turn then will be our delight,
Till by turning, turning, we come 'round right.

—Shaker hymn

More Tenkans

A Weighty Tenkan

After turning *tenkan* around a staff or a balloon or a string, try turning a series of *tenkans* while holding a 10- to 20-pound weight in the turning hand.

Walking Tenkan

Walk across the mat or the room, turning *tenkan* several times in the course of the walking. Compare the degree of stability or difficulty of turning *tenkan* with:

a)   Wide-based, "leaping feet," or

b)   Feet directly under One-Point.

c)   Widely swinging arms, or

d)   Arm thrust forward from the sides but held close to body and One-Point.

Roller Tenkan

On skates or a bicycle (using good sense and protective gear as necessary) try turning in a circle while:

1.   Looking in the direction you are going.

2.   Looking at your hand.

3.   Looking outside of the circle (that is, if turning to the left, look to the right).

4.   Looking in the direction you came from.

5.   Looking at the center point of the circle.

6.   Which is easier?

Repeat the above on the mat.

For *nage* which *tenkan* is easier to do?

For *uke*, which *tenkan* feels more compelling?

Verbal Tenkan

See Dobson (1987).

Yes and No

In pairs, as *nage* extends Unbendable Arm.

1. *Uke* tests as *nage* says: "No, no, no!" Observe the results.

2. *Uke* tests as *nage* says: "Yes, yes, yes!" Observe the results.

Many attempts at self-defense are essentially cries of "No, no!" and a pushing away — when the push is very fast and hard it is known as a punch or a kick.

Aikido says "Yes! Yes!" and draws closer. Aikido techniques may fail if *nage* tries to hold *uke* at arm's length, at a "safe" distance. This appears safer, but is not. Step 2 of many a technique could be phrased as "Give *uke* a hug." This appears more dangerous, but is not. The perception of safety or danger is in the mind. And just as you can choose to be angry or not angry, you can choose to be afraid or not afraid. The danger (or lack of it) is the same, although attitude can often increase or decrease the danger.

I once saw a man wandering through the street drunk or on drugs. Passersby observed him with a watchful calm that offered him no point of focus until one young woman panicked. "Get away from me!" she shrieked, and darted wildly about in confusion. Her noise, random motion, and terror made her everyone's focal point — and his. He set off in hot pursuit. She was grateful to be rescued but others did not need rescuing, due not to size, martial arts training, or weapons — but attitude.

The attacker is amazingly dependent on the "victim."

Light Swords and Fire Hoses

When doing any technique, imagine light or energy streaming out of your fingers like water from a fire hose. If you can't quite imagine that yet, letting water drip into an imaginary bucket works too.

When doing a technique, do it with a light sword, whether you are holding a real sword or not. We use swords in our practice in part because they are a traditional weapon and in larger part because they make "extending *ki*" visible. So would a fire hose.

Ikkyo-Undo*

Ikkyo-undo (the "first-exercise) is yet another way of aligning with *uke*'s energy, matching speed and direction.

With *nage* in *hanmi*,

1. Hips shift forward.

2. Arms swing forward and up, fingers extended, stopping at forehead level.

3. Arms drop to sides, hands softly closed.

4. Hips shift back.

The pattern is: hips-hands, hands-hips.

Uke can test, with *nage* static or in motion:

a) Pushing forward from the small of the back.

b) Pushing into and perpendicular to the chest.

c) For Unbendable Arm (with *nage* standing still).

Once the rhythm is mastered, repeat the exercise while *uke*:

a) Strikes *shomen-uchi* (see page 107) with hand.

b) Strikes *shomen-uchi* with a plastic bat.

(Staffs or swords are also used, but a plastic baseball bat is roughly equivalent to the traditional bundle of bamboo. It's noisy when *ikkyo* is incorrect, but causes no harm — and *ikkyo* improves *immediately*.)

This is the exercise that brought me into Aikido. Karate students are taught to block the most ferocious overhead blows with forearms and so students spend years with sore, injured arms. "Isn't there a better way?" they ask. "Which would you rather have," instructors retort sternly, "a broken arm? or a broken head?" (These are the choices? — not in the Japanese tradition where blocking a sword strike with an arm will leave you with more than a broken arm or head — or less.)

After spending weeks observing classes to see how these people were "faking" the throws and falls, I saw an attacker came in with a heavy stick in an overhead strike that could easily have smashed an arm. But he never reached his target; nage came gliding in, blended with the motion, threw uke and even ended up with the stick. At that point I no longer cared if it was faking — teach me how to fake like that! They did.

Ikkyo With Attitude

Like everything else in Aikido, the success of *ikkyo-undo* depends upon inner attitude. Experiment with the following (*nage* actually saying the words aloud while doing *ikkyo*):

a) "No! No! No!"

b) "Yes! Yes! Yes!"

c) Greeting the attack with a cheery "Hello there! *Thank you* for the opportunity to practice my Aikido . . ."

(See "Yes and No" on page 129.)

Notice how the position of *uke*'s arm changes depending on whether he is modeling fear ("*Uh, oh!*") or welcome.

Two-Direction Exercise*

This exercise (*zengo-undo*) involves a series of turns, reversing direction. When applied to Aikido techniques, it models a response to attacks from two or more attackers coming from opposite directions. It also models demands from two different jobs or chores that threaten to divide time and attention.

Turn completely, directing *ki*, mind, and attention, strongly forward while remaining balanced and centered. Pattern is "hips-hands-hands-hips."

In left *hanmi*, hands lightly closed into fists and arms hanging naturally at sides,

1. At count of "One," shift hips forward, then swing arms up, opening hands and extending fingers.

2. At count of "Two," drop arms back down to sides, closing hands softly; shift hips back. On balls of feet, pivot 180 degrees.

3. At count of "Three," repeat Step 1, shifting hips forward, then swing arms up, opening hands and extending fingers.

4. At count of "Four," repeat Step 2, swinging arms back down to sides, closing hands into soft fists; shift hips back. On balls of feet, pivot 180 degrees.

Uke count aloud, calling "Stop!" at any point. Test by:

a) Pushing straight back on chest.

b) Pushing straight forward at upper or lower back.

c) Checking for Unbendable Arm.

d) Attempting to lift *nage* from ankle.

Eight-Way Exercise*

The Eight-Way Exercise (*happo-undo*) is *ikkyo-undo* (page 130) or *zengo-undo* ("Two-Direction Exercise*" on page 134) with a series of turns in "eight" different directions. Like *zengo-undo,* it models multiple attacks, but from two or more directions.

As in *zengo-undo,* the point is to turn completely, to direct *ki,* mind, and attention strongly forward while remaining balanced and centered. The temptation is to leave your mind behind, to split your attention, to be overcome by second thoughts, regrets, the accumulated weaknesses of small failures. Continuing through a series of turns, *nage* typically becomes more and more unstable, usually falling backwards in response to a test to the chest, having left mind behind.

Mechanically, this is a very simple exercise, and hopelessly baffling to beginners trying it for the first time. Think of moving through eight directions of the compass:

1. North-South,
2. East-West,
3. Southwest-Northeast,
4. Northwest-Southeast.

Or in a room,

1. Front-back,
2. Left side-right side,
3. Corner, corner,
4. Corner, corner.

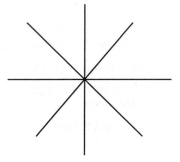

The footwork indicated is simply this:

"Left-right," "left-right," "left-right," "left-right."

If you are an advanced student who has forgotten how confusing this is to beginners, do the exercise backwards (stepping *back* on the *ikkyo* motion rather than forward).

LF = Left Foot. RF = Right Foot.

In left *hanmi* (left foot forward)

1. Step forward with **LF**.

    Swing arms up into *ikkyo* then down.

2. Turn right 180 degrees stepping into right *hanmi* (**RF** forward).

    Swing arms up into *ikkyo* then down.

3. Turn left 90 degrees stepping into left *hanmi* (**LF** forward).

    Swing arms up into *ikkyo* then down.

4. Turn right 180 degrees stepping into right *hanmi* (**RF** forward).

    Swing arms up into *ikkyo* then down.

5. Turn left 45 degrees stepping into left *hanmi* (**LF** forward).

    Swing arms up into *ikkyo* then down.

6. Turn right 180 degrees stepping into right *hanmi* (**RF** forward).

    Swing arms up into *ikkyo* then down.

7. Turn left 90 degrees stepping into left *hanmi* (**LF** forward).

    Swing arms up into *ikkyo* then down.

8. Turn right 180 degrees stepping into right *hanmi* (**RF** forward).

    Swing arms up into *ikkyo*; hold position. *Uke* test.

Variations

Step through the exercise as follows:

a) Feet only, to establish direction and rhythm. When comfortable with these,

b) Add the hands. When feet and arms are working together,

c) Start on the right foot.

d) Start in odd directions or with eyes closed to eliminate dependence on a particular wall or direction.

Attention

Because attention follows or is determined by the eyes, Aikido considers eye direction to be extremely important. Eyes looking one direction and body moving in another usually indicates a split between mind and body, shattered attention, and decreased concentration and strength.

On the mat, experiment with the following:

1. Listening to a speaker while looking elsewhere. *Uke* test.

2. Repeating any physical exercise, such as "Arm Swinging*" (page 70) or "Spinning*" (page 71). Directing eyes and attention in odd directions away from the path of the body. *Uke* test and compare with properly directed eyes.

3. *Not* looking to see who has just come in the dojo door.

In daily life, practice with the following:

1. Giving full, direct attention to a speaker.

2. Giving full, direct attention to a task at hand.

3. Concluding conversations completely before leaving.

   (In this country, a gradual departure is a gentle way of signaling that a conversation is over. The Japanese have a handy and more direct technique for indicating the end of an encounter — a polite bow).

In the "Three-Minute Ki Exercise for Health" (Appendix B) the most common error is in the direction of the eyes.

The consequences of incorrect focus become quickly apparent if the exercise is done while *walking*. Failure to coordinate mind, body, eyes, and focus will leave the perpetrator dizzy and disoriented.

Hollywood Monster

Movie monsters, vampires, and bad guys use a standard Attack Pose of stiffly outstretched arms, with convulsively twitching fingers reaching for the victim's throat. It may look impressive, but is actually an extremely weak attack. Here is a surprising combination of *ki* extension — and applied physics.

With *nage* in *seiza*, *uke* standing,

1. *Nage* extends arms and *ki*.

2. *Uke* reaches for *nage*'s shoulders at base of neck.

3. *Nage* touches *uke*'s arms as *uke* reaches in. While extending *ki*, *nage* gently presses *uke*'s arms slightly upward.

    Notice how extremely dependent *uke* is on *nage*'s every movement. If *nage* shifts arms to the side *uke* will fall.

Variations:

a) *Nage* sitting cross-legged (less stable than *seiza*).

b) With two or three or more *experienced ukes* pushing, one behind the other.

"It's just leverage," they always say.

Leverage is indeed important (see "Ki Door" on page 103) but try it *without* extending.

Ki Breathing

Ki Breathing

Since we all breathe, what could be more natural? What could be more absurd than *studying* how to breathe? In fact, correct healthy breathing is rare. Health problems due to faulty breathing are common and well-documented in the medical literature.

Incorrect ("paradoxical") breathing can actually strain muscles of the neck and torso. These, in turn, entrap nerves producing such side effects as dizziness and headaches, chest and arm pain, or numb fingers.

Breath control is considered so basic in disciplines from singing to yoga to martial arts, that it is studied formally — what can you possibly control if you can't control your own breathing? Breathing exercises can be used for relaxation, autosuggestion, and the formation or modification of habits and behavior. Because breathing is automatic, semi-automatic, and unconscious, it is considered as a bridge to the subconscious and unconscious levels of mind. This bridge can be used to internalize the concepts and sensations developed during *ki* testing.

Oxygen is a nutrient. *Ki* breathing allows you to take in more oxygen and expel more carbon dioxide than is possible during incorrect or even normal breathing. It improves mind and body coordination, increases energy, and enhances confidence. It can even provide such unlikely benefits as improved eyesight — deep breathing is an old astronomer's trick that enables the eye to see fainter stars than are normally detectable by the unaided (or oxygen-depleted) eye.

You can practice breathing in any position, even walking or driving. The traditional *seiza* posture is preferred in Aikido, as it does not compress the abdomen and diaphragm as do other positions. If *seiza* is difficult for you, try using a *seiza* stool or cushions, or sitting erect in a firm chair. You may also sit cross-legged on a comfortable but firm surface, although this tends to compress the diaphragm more than other positions. Nevertheless, be comfortable (though not to the point of collapse or drowsiness). The point of *ki* breathing practice is *breathing* — *not* overcoming physical discomfort by sheer iron will and grim determination.

The standard perception of breathing found throughout the martial arts is that exhalation is "strong" and inhalation is "weak." This is one of the reasons for the powerful exhalation of breath and piercing sound (*kiai*).

Aikido, as usual, sees things a bit differently and strives for strength and power at all points in the cycle of breath.

To establish a baseline for observation, begin by observing your breathing as it is now. Notice the following.

☐ The inward and outward flow of air.

☐ The feel of air in your nostrils, in your mouth and throat; the sound and sensation it makes in your head and chest.

☐ How far a breath goes down inside your body.

☐ Whether you can pay attention to your breathing and still let it operate automatically.

☐ Any tendency towards partial, incomplete, skipped, or forced breaths.

☐ The amount of time you can extend an exhalation or an inhalation.

☐ The amount of time you can hold a breath.

☐ That you can inhale or exhale at will; that you can "hold your breath" with lungs full, partly full, or empty.

Notice also that you must eventually resume breathing whether you want to or not. Rather than fighting that mechanism, use it to learn that volition is best seen as "latitude within limits."

— *Ben Swett*

Practice of Ki Breathing

Begin *ki* breathing by practicing for 5 minutes at a time, working up to 10 or 20 minutes. Work towards a goal of a minimum of 30 minutes, ideally at the same time (or times) each day.

Tohei recommends breathing for 15 minutes before sleeping and 15 minutes after getting up in the morning.

1. **Neutral position**: Sit in *seiza* with lower back curved in, leaning slightly forward. Place your mind at your One-Point. Take a full breath, then . . . .

2. **Exhalation**: Exhale slowly through your mouth. Use a soft *haaaaa* sound. This gently controls the flow of breath with the back of the tongue. Spread the exhalation out over 20 seconds or more.

   When you can exhale no more, bend slightly forward from your One-Point. This compresses the diaphragm and allows you to exhale any remaining air.

3. **Neutral position** (5 seconds): Focus on One-Point.

   When out of air, imagine that you are still exhaling, that breath and *ki* are extending out to the ends of the universe and beyond, but curving into a return path.

4. **Inhalation** (20 seconds): Inhale by closing your mouth and inhaling through your nose. When you can inhale no more, return to Neutral Position.

5. **Neutral position** (5 seconds): Concentrating on your One-Point, imagine that you are still drawing in breath and *ki*, that these are circling around your One-Point, gradually curving into a path from which they will travel out.

   When you can inhale no more, lean back slightly from your One-Point. This expands the diaphragm and allows you to take in a bit more air.

Breathe out so that your breath travels to heaven; breathe in till the breath reaches your belly.

— *Koichi Tohei*

Cloud of Ki

When inhaling and exhaling, imagine that your can see your *ki* flowing in and out with your breath.

If you have trouble visualizing breath, take advantage of cold winter air to see your breath as an actual, rather than an imaginary, cloud.

Rising and Falling Breath

Here is a tool for translating the invisible into the visible.

Standing or seated,

1. Exhale completely and place hand at level of One-Point.

2. Inhale, imagining air filling your body from One-Point up.

3. As your body fills with air, raise your hand to follow the level of the air, as if your hand were floating on top of it.

4. Exhale, letting your hand drop as the level of the air drops.

Switch focus. Rather than the hand following the level of the air, let the level of the air follow the position of the hand.

Beginners encounter a sense of panic similar, in part, to what an asthma sufferer experiences in not being able to have a full breath on demand. This exercise is a means of putting yourself on a "breath budget."

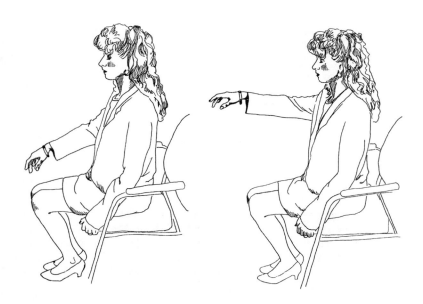

Expansion and Contraction

Changing size is the first step to changing point of view and there is nothing more valuable than a different point of view. The ancient oriental art of *bonsai*, the training and culture of dwarf trees, was originally developed by Buddhist monks as an aid to such exercise.

1. On inhalation, imagine your self expanding — doubling in size at each stage.

2. On exhalation, imagine your self contracting — shrink by half, half, half at each stage.

3. On inhalation, expand out and out. See your breath as light, filling your body, the building, the county, the country, the world, passing the planets, past the solar system, the galaxies, the ends of the universe. When you have expanded as large as you can imagine, imagine sending *ki* as an arrow of light, a jet, a seagull, that disappears over the horizon.

4. On exhalation, contract in to your body, then passing your body. Focus down to your skin, then on individual cells, molecules, atoms, and atomic particles.

Many Aikido techniques involve expansion or contraction. In kokyu-dosa you want to expand, to become larger and larger until your circle takes in your partner's circle. In a grab, you typically want to become smaller and smaller, enabling yourself to move with ease within uke's grasp, within your own skin. For an actual visual example of this exercise, see the movie "Powers of Ten." See also "Changing Size" on page 51.

Stopping Ki or Circling Ki

In *seiza*, while breathing,

1. Imagine sending *ki* out with your breath. Stop the breath for the 5-second resting period, then reverse the flow to breathe in. *Uke* test.

2. Imagine sending *ki* out with your breath, but during the 5-second rest period, imagine it circling around (several times if necessary) before returning. *Uke* test.

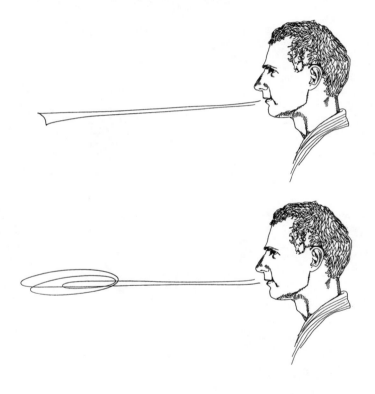

Hal Singer tells of a favorite hill where he took his dog. While his dog ran and played, Hal would sit and practice his ki *breathing imagining that his breath and* ki *went out and out, curving around the earth and then — hit him in the back of the head.*

Breathing With a Bell

As an aid to envisioning your breath traveling out into the distance, practice breathing with a resonant bell. As the waves of sound travel off into the distance, follow them with your mind and breath.

Meditation

Meditation

Ueshiba (like others such as Methodist Founder John Wesley) astonished his followers by arising at 4 a.m. every morning to pray and meditate.[9] Aside from the daily morning miracle of sunrise, there is nothing magical about the hour of 4 a.m. except this: someone willing to leave the comfort of a warm bed at that hour is not playing or dabbling, but is in very serious pursuit of a goal and will achieve corresponding results. What are these results?

- ☐ Solitude in the midst of confusion.
- ☐ Time with yourself and with God.
- ☐ Patterning of goals, images, and activities.
- ☐ Marked shift in perception of time.
- ☐ Calm and relaxation.

The practice of meditation is often urged just for relaxation. But what is the benefit of relaxation? Not being tense? A good thing, but there's more. Relaxation induces an *alpha* state, considered by many to be best for learning and patterning.[10]

---

[9] Because of its association with Eastern religions, meditation is viewed by some Christian fundamentalists as an Eastern heresy. In fact, it is recognized by all the great world religions, including Judaism and Christianity (both originally "Eastern religions"). It is mentioned repeatedly in both the Old and New Testaments and throughout the writings of the great saints. On the secular side, Freud and especially Jung recognized the importance of meditation in one form or another.

[10] *Alpha* refers to the frequency of the brain's electrical activity of 8 to 13 hertz (cycles per second). Biofeedback machines and tapes are widely available but expensive compared to simply closing the eyes. On the other hand, you may want to experiment with an "electronic *uke*." There are many electronic biofeedback devices on the market today; inexpensive ones are available through various scientific-novelty stores. Ordinarily, a range of tones indicates a range of relaxed or stressed states. Experiment with raising and lowering the tone. What happens to the tone when *uke* begins to test? At what tone are you more stable? Less stable? Can you raise or lower the tone at will?

The following exercises feature not only imagery, but changes in point of view. Some are done while sitting quietly alone. Others can be done throughout the course of the day while immersed in the stream of "real life."

Tohei offers these principles for character development:

- [ ] Develop a Universal Mind.
- [ ] Love and protect all you meet.
- [ ] Show gratitude for all you have.
- [ ] Do good in secret (*entoku*) without expectation of reward.
- [ ] Have soft eyes and a composed manner.
- [ ] Be large-hearted and forgiving.
- [ ] Think deeply and see clearly.
- [ ] Maintain a spirit of unshakeable composure.
- [ ] Be vigorous and energetic.
- [ ] Persevere.

Much of the groundwork for these characteristics is laid in quiet, meaningful meditation.

Counting

This deceptively simple exercise may reveal just how busy and cluttered our minds can be. You may find it very difficult to do on the first try.

1. Relax, clear your mind, and then count slowly to ten and back to one, thinking only of the number.

2. When you find your thoughts wandering, stop and begin again.

Got it? Now repeat from one to 100 and back again.

The Grid

Imagine your body as a mesh of fine charged wire, an energy grid, or a cloud of electrons.

Rather than resisting oncoming energy, let it pass through you as easily as the wind blowing through a wire fence.

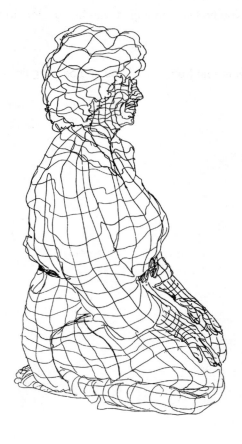

This seemingly solid body that sits at my seemingly solid desk is a swirling cloud of electrons and other infinitesimally small particles. In one atom, the spaces between nucleus and electrons are like the spaces between sun and planets. We are indeed mostly space. This exercise asks that you imagine that reality as reality.

The Gridlock

This is the *real* "on the street."

As many have discovered, it is very easy to maintain One-Point and good will towards men in the peace and serenity of the *dojo*, a *ki* class, a convent, a meditation garden. But most of us must return to the real world, perhaps by way of heavy traffic — a daunting challenge to the relaxed life. In the Washington, D.C. area alone there are over 900 cars per square mile and their drivers, with their own perceptions, attitudes, traditions, misconceptions, inexperience, and possibly alcohol or drugs — a volatile mix. In this area alone, more than 16,000 motorists a year are charged with driving under the influence of alcohol or drugs; in 1994 these factors led to over 6,600 crashes and 130 fatalities. Nationwide, more than 110 people are killed, and 5,700 injured on the roads every day.

Teens comprise 7 percent of drivers, but cause 28 percent of highway injuries, nine times the rate of older drivers. Forty percent of teenage deaths occur on the highways. Death rates for young American men actually dropped during the Viet Nam war as young men were removed from the roads to the relative safety of guns and grenades.

Some attribute our collective madness on the highway to our identification with our cars. The protective anonymity of tons of steel and tinted windows tempt us to behave in ways that we never would otherwise. "*I am* my expensive and prestigious luxury car — You want *me* to move over to let *you* pass?"

Yet according to AAA, 85 to 95 percent of crashes are caused by driver error, from honest mistakes, not by hostile people looking for a wrangle. Nevertheless, those who assume hostile intent and retaliate end up in a back-and-forth dance that can end in disaster. While many of us study martial arts for safety "on the street," we seem oblivious to danger "on the road." Better to wear a seat belt, drive kindly and sensibly, and practice inner calm.

In Aikido, contests and competitions are forbidden. While competition helps to build skill, Aikido techniques are based on the theory of non-dissension. Failure to grasp the theory means failure to master the techniques. Tohei urges those who want contests and matches to compete with themselves.

A person who likes contests and matches should try having one with himself. For instance, a quick-tempered man might say, "Today I'm not going to get angry once." If he manages to hold his temper all day, he wins; if he does not, he loses. If we make progress without causing anyone else trouble and without bearing ill will against anyone, we will get to the point where we are always winning. That is real victory. If we fail to win over ourselves, even though we win over others, we are doing nothing but satisfying our own conceit and vanity.

There is hardly a better arena for such an internal contest than on the road. Use rush-hour traffic to practice blending, flowing, extension of good will, and *ma-ai* ("correct distance") in the car just as in other physical vehicles. Practice not reacting, not wasting energy ascribing ulterior motives to the speeder who zooms up from behind flashing his lights and honking for you to get out of the way. Note any emotional reactions and consider the following.

- ☐ If a boulder or a lion were hurtling towards you would you waste time feeling huffy? — or just get out of the way?

- ☐ Notice your shoulders. Are they up around your ears? Drop them. Breathe.

- ☐ Instead of being angry because someone cut in, can you be pleased that you blended well, avoiding injury, higher insurance costs, and legal entanglements for both of you?

- ☐ Must you always speed up to pass? Notice that you can also fall back. Blend.

- ☐ Must you be angry? Your anger will not make a bit of difference to an oblivious offender — but it *will* affect you.

- ☐ Can you take someone who is stuck in traffic, trying to make a left turn, under your protection? If not, why not?

- ☐ Recall incidents in traffic and your reaction to them. *Uke* test. Observe how *old* some of these memories are.

- ☐ Observe the *time* factor involved in your reactions. What is the actual elapsed time that defines traffic as "moving well" versus actual elapsed time that causes impatience, rage, and fury? How much of this time and how much of your reaction depends on the space of time *you chose* to allow for travel?

☐ If you are a physically small human disturbed by bullying tactics or lack of consideration by others, observe your own behavior when in a large powerful vehicle and faced with pedestrians.

If you are a physically large human, walk across a large busy intersection, and observe how it feels to be a pedestrian walking in company with 3,000-pound bodies that assume greater size, strength, and speed give them the right of way.

Notice that behavior is not a function of vehicle design but of the driving spirit.

☐ While it is easy to rage about other people's conduct on the road, try this contest for the competitive soul: can you make it home or over [X] miles without committing a single error of judgment or of courtesy? Here are the rules of the game:

1. Obey the speed limit.

2. Dedicate yellow lights to drivers attempting to turn left rather than speeding up and zooming through yourself.

3. Signal all turns and lane changes, planning ahead rather than cutting in or out, or braking at the last minute.

4. Yield to pedestrians.

5. Obey all traffic signals (including red lights, No Turn On Red, and Yield signs).

6. Assume confusion or insanity rather than malice.

   Although increasingly rare in practice, not one of these is anything other than standard motor vehicle law or good sense, whether operating a vehicle of steel and plastic or one of flesh and bone.

The emotional hook of perceived hostile intent is often worse than the action itself. I once lost all patience with a driver who was weaving unsteadily down the road. My perception changed radically when the driver made a clumsy left-hand turn from the middle lane — into the hospital emergency room.

Thomas Merton recounts an old tale of "the empty boat." If an empty, drifting boat bumps up against a boatman on the river, even a bad-tempered man will not lose his temper, but simply deal with the situation. If a boat with a man in it does exactly the same thing in exactly the same way, the boatman will scream and curse. But what has changed?

I Am

As mentioned in "The Gridlock," people behave in strange and different ways when wrapped in a coccoon of steel and anonymity. Perceived threats to personal dignity, personal rights, or prowess turn deadly especially when the power, speed, model, style, and dollar value of the particular vehicle being driven become strangely confused with personal identity.

In fact, you are to your body as your body is to your car. Neither is really you.

This classic yoga meditation is an aid to defining the difference.

1. Make a list of all the things that you "are."

2. Gently peel away the defining mask. For example,

    "I am a man." No, that is the physical vehicle that I inhabit.

    "I am a mother." No, that is the current job description that I fill.

    "I am a fraid." No, that is a current state of emotion.

    "I am . . .

Imagine that you have lost your wallet, all identifying paperwork, your resume, all belongings, all contact with friends, family, your previous world. Who are you? What do you do?

Mudra of Mind-Body Unification

A *mudra* is a hand position, used in meditation, that helps to achieve the very thing that it symbolizes. In *seiza*,

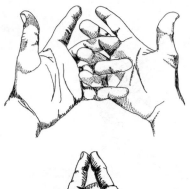

1. Fold fingers together as shown. The tips of each pair of fingers touch; thumbs cross, left over right, to touch the bases of the index fingers.

2. Raise fingers to eye level.

3. Imagine *ki* streaming from your One-Point up through your body, out your arms, and through the fingers as if through the nozzle of a fire hose.

159

4.   *Uke* test. Compare the stability of this pose with other tests done in the ordinary *seiza* position.

5.   Lower the arms, fingers still joined in the *mudra*, to a natural and relaxed sitting position. *Uke* test.

The Light Bubble

An exercise for expanding *ki*.

1. Imagine a warm spark of light at your One-Point.

2. Imagine what light would look like if it were a liquid.

3. Imagine expanding this light outward, surrounding yourself with such a substance. Extend the bubble below your feet and above your head. To help with this imagery, trace a circle with your finger as far as you can reach.

4. Pay special attention to your back, turning within the bubble to check that area and any holes or weak spots.

5. Firm up the outer skin of your light bubble (6 inches to a foot thick) to the consistency of soft rubber — so that slings and arrows, dark words and looks can't enter to the inner core.

6. Have *uke* test gently at *nage*'s request throughout the course of construction of this bubble.

Happy or Sad

Consider the effect of focusing on happy or sad images, on calm or violent images.

Uke test while *nage* looks at:

1. A happy or cheerful picture.
2. A sad or unhappy picture.

    The pictures may be as simple as the sketches below.

The first time I saw this demonstrated, in a speech class, the group reacted with shock, outrage, and shouted *fury* — it simply could not, *must not* be true. They were particularly angry and frightened because it did work so very well.

And it was so simple. Do things have to be difficult to be effective?

— *George Simcox*

Morihei Ueshiba Meets Rube Goldberg

The common vision of the martial artist is that of a hard-eyed, hard-bitten, potential killer. Someone *very very* serious. Aikido preaches "soft eyes, loving protection, and a large heart." Zen tradition is filled with tales of wise old "fools" of impish and zany humor. Jay Gluck witnessed one of the best, an encounter between *O-Sensei* and cartoonist Rube Goldberg. (See Gluck, 1992).

Rube was visiting Japan. He strolled into the *Aikikai Hombu Dojo* stepping up onto the elevated floor "with a huge cigar protruding from his maw like a naval cannon" — and his shoes on. As horrified students raced to remove Rube's shoes, O-Sensei heard the commotion and came out to investigate. "As his eyes met Rube's O-Sensei's eyebrows rose. His eyes lit up. His straggly beard vibrated. *'Haw!'* he hawed."

Pushing Rube's interpreter aside, he grabbed the befuddled little man by the arm and hauled him, cigar "streaming smoke like dragon spoor," into the sacred *tokonoma* alcove. *O-Sensei* shouted orders. Startled students raced for their practice weapons and attacked, screaming. *O-Sensei* stood in the middle of the vortex whirling, ducking, spinning as bodies flew everywhere. Then it was over. Rube walked out of the alcove, "laughed and tugged *O-Sensei's* wispy white beard."

> *O-Sensei . . . pulled the immense stogie out of Rube's mouth, bopped him on the head with it, jammed it back into his mouth and laughed. Rube guffawed. They both laughed like the ancient fools. Then both turned and left. Not a word had been uttered.*

I had never heard this story before, nor had anyone else I mentioned it to. Thinking it might be a charming fiction that I had taken all too seriously, I wrote author Jay Gluck. He replied:

"I assure you the Zen Fools episode involving *O-Sensei* and Rube is history. *No one present realized the significance of the strange scene.* Other witnesses I questioned months later were interested only in the fact that they had been granted the honor of tangling with their 'angel of God' like a gaggle of Jacobs. None of the Japanese knew *who* or *what* the funny looking man in the porkypie hat and stogie was. As he told me when I questioned him some months later, *O-Sensei* recognized *what* he was — *from his eyes.*"

Dark Side

What you think and where you place your mind matters. It matters more than most of us will ever know.

1. *Uke* test while *nage* listens to:

    a)   The 11:00 news or an article read from a lurid tabloid.

    b)   A report of an example of goodness, wise kindness.

    c)   Favorite music (various examples).

2. Repeat while *nage* thinks about:

    a)   What a terrible day it was.

    b)   What a great day it was, or,

    c)   An example of a single good thing from the apparently terrible day considered above.

Avoid spiteful gossip, sensationalism, and those who revel in dirt, dishonor, and scandal. Test the difference between *noting* the fact that someone has made a mistake and *enjoying* the fact that someone has made a mistake. The first may be a statement of fact. The latter is an all-too-effective means of "tuning the spirit" (see "The Spiritual Spectrum" on page 172) to the dark side. These tests reveal the options and the consequences of your point of view. Choose. You will carry that choice with you throughout the day and throughout life.

Jesus said "If thine eye causeth thee to sin, pluck it out," a Hard Saying that seems to make little practical sense. But in the original Greek, the word used is *ophthalmos*. It meant the physical eye but it also meant "point of view." Does your point of view cause you to be dark and negative? Better to change it than to fill yourself with darkness.

Finally, brethren, whatsoever things are true, whatsoever things are honest, whatsoever things are just, whatsoever things are pure, whatsoever things are lovely, whatsoever things are of good report; if there be any virtue, and if there be any praise, think on these things.

— Philippians 4:8

Radio and TV

What you see and what you dwell on becomes part of you. There is a thin line between simply observing your surroundings and taking what you observe as ideal, as fact, as normal behavior, as reality. Much has been said about the effect of the media on children, as if adults are somehow immune. This is simply not so.

On Halloween, 1938, Orson Welles' Mercury Theater of the Air presented H. G. Wells' *War of the Worlds*, a tale of a Martian invasion of Earth. Many listeners reported being frightened on hearing the apparent special news announcements — then switching to other stations and realizing what they were actually hearing.[11] All should have been clear within a few minutes — the first half ends with the world overcome by Martian craft and their poisonous gas. Second half: tales of the survivors which could only be dramatic material. Nevertheless, there was mass panic and even suicide.

In the aftermath, the program and its effect on listeners was cited as an example of the power of radio over human minds and emotions. Its effect was due to excellent scripting and acting.[12] Today, faced with even better special effects and visual media, we like to believe that no such power exists. Merchandisers, who know better, spend billions on advertising. In Aikido, we see the *War of the Worlds* effect every day — with only a slightly longer time frame.

Many come to Aikido classes to train for safety "on the street." As noted, "on the street" *usually* means "as seen on TV or in the movies" and it is *mostly* bunk. With every terrifying new martial arts movie, we see a surge of terrified new students. They want arm-breaking techniques, killing blows to the spine. They are terribly

---

[11] The real essence of the Scientific Method. My old geology prof boiled down all the pages devoted to that topic in every beginning science book to just this: *"How do you know?"* i.e, "Aieeee! We're being invaded by Martians!" "How do you know?" "Because Orson Welles on the regular weekly science fiction Mercury Theatre of the Air says so." "Hmm. What do other information sources have to say?"

[12] It was *not* due to the novelty of radio as radio was no longer a novelty. The first radio news broadcast aired in 1916, the first paid radio commercials in 1922. NBC was founded in 1926 and CBS in 1928, 10 years before the supposed "invasian" by Martians.

disappointed when, instead, we teach them how to roll, how to turn. We have even had to bar some students from classes because of their insistence and persistence in trying dirtied-up versions of techniques on their classmates. They are afraid because they believe what they have seen on the screen: that psychopathic killers lurk behind every bush and the monster never dies. (See Ebert, 1994.)

It is extremely useful to remember that the programming itself is not the point. It is there only to get you to buy the ticket or to watch the commercials.[13] The best way to hook a customer is to give him something he wants or needs or thinks he needs. The best way to do that, as many dealers know, is to create an addiction.

It is advertising wisdom that "sex sells." So does an enjoyable surge of adrenaline. A program that can hook the viewer on his own brain chemicals is assured of an audience. Notice the current emphasis on revenge: [X] did [Y] to [Z] "and now he's out for revenge!" An even better formula is *justified* contempt and revenge. Presenting a bad guy who murders priests and nuns or helpless young girls distances the viewer from our standards of justice and frees him to believe in a cruel monster who deserves anything he gets. Problem is that the bad guy is fictional. The emotions are real and serve as future templates for thought, example, and behavior.

Watch for the hooks in programming and advertising.

1. Which emotions does the presentation attempt to manipulate or stimulate and how is this done?

2. For commercials, what are the implied benefits if you buy?

3. What is the underlying spirit? and where does it lie on the Spiritual Spectrum?

The essential is to excite the spectators. If that means playing Hamlet on a flying trapeze or in an aquarium, you do it.

— Orson Welles

---

[13] In 1928, William Paley, 27-year-old advertising manager of his father's cigar company, signed a $50-per-week advertising contract — while Dad was safely away on vacation. Young Paley was roundly criticized for his extravagance, but when cigar sales soared he cut out the middleman and founded Columbia Broadcasting System (CBS).

Treasures

Make a list of five specific events or situations that were wrong, unfair, unkind, mean, spiteful, or cruel. These may be things you have experienced or seen yourself, read about in the paper, or seen on the news.

1.

2.

3.

4.

5.

Meditate on these. Note mood. When ready, have *uke* test.

Now list five specific events or situations that were right, just, wisely kind, good, and beautiful.

1.

2.

3.

4.

5.

Meditate on these. Note your change of mood. When ready, have *uke* test.

If you can't think of five, are you really alive? Now consider: Why is it easier to recall the barbs and slights of others rather than the good done to or for us? If true for you, change it.

— *George Simcox*

Notice that you yourself caused depression or elevation of spirit by choosing what to think about, what to dwell on. This is the power of positive or negative thinking, the source of your power over yourself and over those things that come into your circle of influence.

— *Ben Swett*

Treasure Chest

Perhaps starting with the items mentioned in the previous exercise, make a longer and more complete list of things that are good and true and beautiful; whatever would inspire you to impartial good-will, love, joy, inner peace, patience, kindness, goodness, faithfulness, gentleness, and self-control. *Uke* test.

Meditating on the good and true and beautiful is not escapist denial of "reality," whatever that may be (see Lewis, C. S. in *Books, Movies and Videos*). It is a means of saving up the treasures of your heart and mind. These are powerful tools in your toolbox; the real magic rings and charms. They have power over demons, those without and within.

This is not to say that all is Truth and Beauty. Denying or ignoring the fact that unpleasant realities exist only makes them stronger by forcing them into the subconscious where they are less easily reached or dealt with. Or, these things remain in consciousness but as lies — to self or to others.

This illusion is taken a step down by the cynic who declares the worst of two possibilities (and its consequences) to be "reality." To the true professional cynic, only the back end of the horse is real. But consider a cut diamond or other faceted gemstone. Which facet ("face") or point of view is the "real" one? Consider a puppy or a baby. Which end is "real?" The one which occasionally causes inconvenience? —or the one remarkable for expressing affection and delight?

The question is an absurdity. The most cuddly of babies or puppies must be fed and trained. But there is far more to a baby than the annoyance of diapers; more responsibility than chortles and hugs.

We do not get to create all reality; reality is what *is*. However, we *can* choose our focus, and this ability to change our point of view is our greatest power.

Acknowledge the reality and act in spite of it.

Point of View

Rolling is a frightening new undertaking for students who have spent lives committed to the vertical plane. There is a tendency to go down, all the while thinking "Oh no! Oh no! Oh no!" In Aikido, this point of view often translates into a misunderstanding of *nage* as winner and *uke* as loser.

If this is a familiar difficulty, try changing your point of view to see a fall as:

1. An opportunity for rolling practice.
2. A back massage from the mat.
3. Flying.
4. A gift of energy from *uke* to help you get back *up*.

Over the years I have been privileged to work with many people of capability, wisdom and good sense. "Colonel Bob" is one of the best at always managing to come up with a positive and practical point of view.

A customer complained that my database program was "crashing the system" (meaning the entire site computer network) because it happened to go down several times while my program was in use. I became impatient with the repeated calls and with what I perceived as foolish accusations.

"No," said my boss. "There is a problem. Whatever the problem may be, the customer believes that you can fix it. And knows that he gets faster response from you than from the Help Desk."

This didn't change the customer, or the technical difficulties that the LAN was experiencing, but it greatly changed my point of view — and patience.

Night workers next door to our dojo *thought us a wicked lot when they heard crashes followed by peals of hilarious laughter. One night they came to see these people who took such delight in slam-dunking their partners then laughing at them. What they found was this: it was the ones who had just been thrown who were laughing.*

Internal Aikido Class

Students of *Ki* Development can go through every exercise in this manual in meditation. Establish One-Point, relax, drop weight underside, and extend *ki*. Note feelings, moods.

Students of Aikido can go through Aikido techniques. Visualize the attack, see the energy, blend with the energy, perform the technique and the hold-down. You will probably find it difficult to maintain concentration for more than a few seconds but the difficulty of doing a technique for two all on your own is a test of real Aikido.

Beginners tend to see techniques as *nage* versus *uke*, a "win-lose" situation. If *nage* throws *uke*, *nage* wins and *uke* "loses." If *uke* is unthrowable, *uke* "wins" and *nage* "loses."

Not so.

Uke "wins" by being a good teacher. The test is not the ability to remain unthrowable. The test is this: Do you understand a technique well enough to guide an unfamiliar *nage* through the technique and the throw? — without the help of *nage*'s presence?

While sitting quietly and comfortably, eyes closed, without losing focus or concentration, go through:

1. An entire attack and technique.

2. A series of attacks and techniques.

3. An entire test series. (The 5th *kyu* test, then the 4th *kyu* test . . . .)

   a) As *nage.*

   b) As *uke.*

      If you lose concentration, go back to the beginning and start again.

At the Merrifield dojo, Steve Kendall is renowned for One-Man Taigi; no partner necessary, he throws himself — including the sankyo hold downs. It's great fun to watch, enormously entertaining, but it also demonstrates a profound understanding of the energy, the flow, balance, timing, and technique.

You can apply this technique to any other activity or sport such as golf — from walking onto the green to the landing and roll of the ball. Or do a dance step, play a piano piece, establish a goal and achieve it step by step, all in meditation.

Harmony and Housework

During classes at the *dojo*, shoes are neatly stored in a rack. At many more traditional schools, they are carefully placed around the mat, facing out. The *samurai* tradition required constant readiness. Inability of a warrior to respond because of a missing sandal or misplaced or faulty weapons would have been an unspeakable shame. The same goal of battle-readiness should apply to modern everyday life.

- ☐ It is wasteful and inefficient to spend half an hour looking for the other shoe.

- ☐ If you are never sure of your checkbook balance, then you're never sure of your weapons, your tools, your resources.

- ☐ An effective encounter with the tax office or returns department is impossible if the records can't be located.

- ☐ Too many material things, their payments and upkeep, mean financial slavery.

- ☐ A huge sinkful of dirty dishes harbors small enemies while making it impossible to brew a cup of tea or cook an egg.

- ☐ Poor planning and poor meals destroy health and life.

After class, the hakama is carefully folded, its pleats tucked into place and the ties intricately woven together. I folded the pleats, as this preserves the creases. But I never learned to fold the ties. Why? Because there is no "Hakama Folding Test" on the test list. Now I think that folding those ties, going through the steps, this small daily ritual of closing, is a wonderful opportunity to do just one thing right, to do it carefully, to do it well.

— CMS

"Who put this book on the shelf upside-down?! There is not anything which is all right to do without presence of mind. Not noticing this kind of thing is where slackness begins. Put things back properly!"

— *Koichi Tohei*

The Way of a Warrior, the Art of Politics, is to stop trouble before it starts. The Way of a Warrior is to establish harmony.

—*Morihei Ueshiba*

Each small task of everyday life is part of the total harmony of the universe.

— *St. Theresa of Lisieux*

The Spiritual Spectrum

Good or Evil is not an Either/Or situation. It is a spectrum[14] of desire and behavior, a continuum ranging from kind to cruel, caring to exploitive, light to dark. These relationships hold true whether the personality is in a body, out of body, coming from the subconscious, or over the telephone as sales pitch.

The practice of evaluating source is "discernment." The practice of choosing source or position is "tuning." Key is attitude toward others. Observe thoughts and desires throughout the day, whether acted on or not. Where do they fit on the spiritual spectrum?

＋ Loves all

Kind, wise, and wisely kind. Trustworthy. Feeding each other. Creative. "Give, not get."

Appreciating and building on the good in self and others. Graciousness and gentleness.

Rejoicing in joys, growth, and progress of others.

Decent, sensible, self-controlled, patient.

Desiring to help, to rescue, to do good.

Ahimsa.

0

Harmless, neutral. Neither doing harm nor desiring to do harm.

Indifferent, uncaring, disinterested.

Self-centered, egocentric, greedy, materialistic.

Blaming, scapegoating, manipulating others for personal gain, appetite. "Get, not give."

Rejoicing in errors, faults, and failures of others. Envious, covetous, spiteful.

Fear-mongering, hate-mongering. Lying, cynical, hateful, abusive, sadistic, cruel, destructive. Feeding on others, predatory, and murderous.

▬ Loves None

---

[14] After Swett (1997).

Right and Revenge

An internal visualization with *uke* testing or in groups of three, acted out by *nage* and two *uke*s.

1. With Unbendable Arm or in *seiza, nage* imagine being jumped by a knife-wielding attacker, applying an Aikido technique, taking control of the knife, and bringing the attacker to the ground in a gentle but effective hold-down. *Uke* test.

2. Enact the same scene, but after taking control of the knife, imagine stabbing and killing the attacker. *Uke* test.

3. Repeat while focusing on the following thoughts:

   a) He deserved it.

   b) This is fun.

   c) This is genuinely necessary to protect another.[15]

The moment of victory is too short to live for that and nothing else.

— *Martina Navratilova*

---

[15] See Dobson's "A Kind Word Turneth Away Wrath" in Heckler (1985) for an example of an apparent desire to protect. What was it really?

Dislike and Hatred

Think of your friends, acquaintances, co-workers. Some you like and admire, others you have chosen to dislike, to hold in contempt, or to hate. List these and your reasons why. What effect do these choices have on you? When you have your list, *uke* test.

To demonstrate that the effects *on* you originate *within you* and your own attitudes, try this on an inanimate object.

1. Observe an inanimate object of annoying design, such as really ugly wallpaper, a clumsy piece of furniture, an old car, a raggedy sneaker or tennis shoe.

2. Consider how ugly it is, and how much you dislike having to be associated with it. *Uke* test.

3. Change your point of view to see this item as an act of creation, clumsy perhaps, but *creative*; perhaps by a child or someone holding a saw for the first time. Run the tape backwards on the old car or old shoe to see all the times that it functioned as a worthy tool in work or play for its owner. *Uke* test.

On renting an apartment from an elderly lady I asked permission to pull down the peeling wallpaper to reveal the beautiful dark wood paneling underneath. Thinking she would be glad of the free handiwork, I was surprised at her hesitation and the look of regret that crossed her face when she reluctantly agreed. I asked her to tell me its story.

During the darkest days of World War II she and her best friend had spent a weekend papering that room, thinking to "brighten things up a bit." I saw ugly fuschia wallpaper, of goofy design, an affront to my personal version of good sense and good taste. She saw a weekend of shared work with a dear friend long dead, and light in the darkness.

While I still would not willingly choose that particular pattern for me, I could not see it quite the same way again.

Give or Get

In the sense of positive or negative orientation, "purpose" can be reduced to the desire to *give* or to *get*. What is the effect on *nage*?

In *seiza* or with Unbendable Arm, *uke* test as *nage* imagines,

1. A choice of getting or giving help:

    a) [*Someone*] must help me.

    b) I will help [*someone*].

2. A job interview from the following perspective:

    b) What can I get from the company?

    c) What can I contribute to the company?

Opportunities to observe orientation of purpose are infinite and often deceptive. On the mat, an offer of instruction may appear to be an offer of help, but it may also be something else. Those in the military and in police organizations are particularly subject to the same temptations and opportunities.

A retired policeman commented on how many of his colleagues had burned out while he had not. What was the difference?

"Point of view," he said. "Many see 'policing' as class monitor, the one to enforce the rules and to bring the rule-breakers to justice. Or they see it as an opportunity to get a cut of the action. Truth is, there will always be an endless tide of rule-breakers. And putting your life on the line for a few more dollars under the table is not a worthwhile trade."

He saw it as an opportunity to protect his family, his street, his city and the good people in it. Not as All-Powerful Protector or Super Cop, but as organizer, helper, team builder. The best protection for a neighborhood invaded by drug dealers was for neighbors to protect one another, to watch, take notes, collect evidence, to work as a team. He taught them how, taught them well, and a neighborhood was saved.

— CMS

Giving is giving only if the other person goes away enriched. If you take pride away from them in order to feed your own view of yourself, the gift you make — even if it's hours of encouragement and support — isn't fair compensation.

— Merle Shain

Ahimsa

Ahimsa, "harmlessness," is a traditional discipline of yoga, but it is much more than the absence of harm or destruction.

It is the absence of *desire* to harm or destroy.

Achieving *ahimsa* is achieving a neutral state, a zero point on the spiritual spectrum.

"Aw, he's harmless," is a strangely derogatory phrase commonly heard in daily life. But in the spiritual sense, harmlessness is no small accomplishment.

We have the opportunity to be harmless day by day, minute by minute. From there, which way?

1. Observe all the passing desires of the heart, whether these are acted upon or not.

2. Note their position on the spiritual spectrum.

Ahimsa can also be thought of as *impartiality*. Here is a "walking meditation" for the practice of impartiality.

On watching contests, sports events, or nature shows:

1. Cheer for one side without becoming emotional over the outcome. *Enjoy* the game, *appreciating* the good catches, good hits performed by skillful players on either side.

2. Change sides at half time.

He causes his sun to rise on the evil and the good, and sends rain to fall on the just and the unjust. Be ye impartial as your Father in heaven is impartial.

— Matthew 5:45, 48

Note that this is a slightly different translation. This excellent advice is usually translated as an exhortation to be "perfect," but the preceding passages (43-47) deal throughout with non-selective goodness, kindness, and graciousness. The Greek word used is *teleioi*, meaning "complete," "mature," "fully-formed," or "not broken into parts" — or as we say in English, "impartial." Compare with Latin *integer*, meaning "whole" or "complete," which became *integrite*, "soundness," "wholeness," — now familiar in English as *integrity*.

Keep *One*-Point.

Entoku

Entoku is "good done in secret." While it benefits the receiver, it also benefits the giver by orienting and tuning position on the spiritual spectrum.

According to the Talmud, the truest kindnesses are those done to animals as they have no means of repayment.

Entoku releases the giver from the hook of desiring feedback, adulation, payment, reward.

Acts of kindness and love may be unremembered by the doer, but they are remembered by others. These gifts and gratitude for them, stored in the minds and memories of others, are the "treasure stored up in heaven." See the review of *Miracle of Mindfulness* (Thich Nhat Hanh, 1987) for an unforgettable kindness done by a nameless old woman under the most amazing circumstances. See Conari Press (1993) for many more. What was the effect on the receiver?

The best portions of a good man's life,
His little, nameless, unremembered acts,
Of kindness and love.
— William Wordsworth

Thank You

In *seiza* or standing,

1.   *Nage* think of resisting the incoming energy. *Uke* test.

2.   *Nage* say "Thank you!" (and mean it!). Accept and think of the incoming energy as a gift. *Uke* test.

Aikido is also the art of "Thank you."

"Yes and yes and thank you, thank you for the opportunity to practice my Aikido!"

Practice saying "Thank you!" verbally and internally at every possible opportunity. The person who taught you to read, the unseen army that keeps water running through your pipes, all the bad things that never happened, all the people who have helped you see something you could not see for yourself.

The ability to say "Thank you" is the first step to appreciation, in turn, the first step in the Exercise of Blessing.

Appreciation

Appreciation is the action of recognizing the value and worth of persons or things — not as they might be, could be, or should be, but as they *are*.

We are told to appreciate others, to realize that everyone has special talents and abilities, but do we? I learned an unforgettable lesson about abilities, strengths, and weaknesses from a soccer game.

One of our players was difficult to appreciate in terms of standard soccer skills. She was slow, plodding, and notoriously lacking in reflexes. Various members had schemed to eject her from the team but could not because of her unfailing faithfulness and reliability. She never missed a practice, never missed a game, and always played valiantly as best she could. Because she was slow and plodding she had to play her position and concentrate on passes rather than wandering all over the field. Because she was not sprinting here and there she never wore herself out or needed to be substituted. "She is not an asset to the team," they said.

One day we met a team that had such a superb dribbler that they never bothered to field more than five or six players, yet they were trouncing the league. Two of our players changed that: our best one and our worst one.

Our best player ignored the feints.

Our "worst" player *never even saw them* — a "failing" that allowed her to consistently and reliably clear the ball while others could not.

Super Dribbler, baffled by this unexpected turn of events, was unable to adapt her strategy, and, because everything had depended on that one skill, she had no team to call on when it failed.

We won because of a completely unexpected combination of skills.

A strength that was a weakness.

A weakness that was a strength.

Good or Ill Will

This exercise and its consequences are traditionally known as "blessing" and "cursing."

Always conclude this exercise on the "blessing" note.

For a group demonstration, send a volunteer out of the room while you explain the test to the group. Test as follows.

1. *Uke* test the volunteer for Unbendable Arm.

    When Unbendable Arm has been obtained,

2. On unspoken signal, group extends ill will towards the volunteer, hope of failure, thinking of everything disliked (real or imagined) about this person. *Uke* test for Unbendable Arm.

3. On unspoken signal, group extend kindness, caring, and good will towards the volunteer. *Uke* test again for Unbendable Arm.

The volunteer *nage* may be tested while facing away from the class in order to *eliminate* visual clues, or facing the class to *include* visual clues.

Do individual demonstrations in groups of four.

1. An *uke* and a *nage* repeat the steps above, *uke* providing the flow of ill or good will towards *nage*.

2. The two other partners test the active *uke* and *nage*.

3. Determine the following:

    a) What is the effect of good or ill will on the person who receives it?

    b) *On the person who sends it?*

The Act of Blessing

1. Stop — Get quiet and let other concerns go.

2. Observe — Focus your attention on a person, pet, or other living thing, either in person or as an image.

3. Appreciate — Notice the good in that being, not as you wish it were, but as it is now.

4. Bless — Send a flow of good will towards the entity.

5. Stop — Release or reduce your caring-connection.

   Uke test the blessed and the blesser.

The connection is what makes this exercise powerful, whether it is called "extending *ki*" or "*ki* healing" or "blessing and prayer."

   a) Most powerful: How can *we* help [this person]?

   b) Most ineffective: Please bless all the poor and homeless, and all the starving children in far-away countries.

   c) Actually harmful: Please make [name] better.

      This holds the built-in assumption and image of the subject as sick. Far better to appreciate and remember the person as healthy and strong.

Rationale

Over the last few years, the Noble Warrior has reappeared in Aikido writings and teachings. The ideal of the Noble Warrior, pledged to serve and protect, is found throughout the world, in all places, in all times. And always the problem has been how to keep the Noble Warrior noble.

The Noble Warrior protects loved ones from hunger, predators, or from each other, carving out a place of order, safety, and decency.

"Budo" said Ueshiba, "is Love." But those with the power to kill face the temptation to exchange the power of love for the love of power. They start as farmers and parents protecting family and fields. They end as surly self-important bureaucrats with swords.

For some, the only reason to stay on the upright path may be shame, fear of punishment, or doctrine. If these are removed, what reason is left? This problem is particularly poignant in current society, much of which preaches a doctrine of "anything goes" and there are no consequences. The very concept of sin or of wrongdoing has fallen badly out of popularity.

Ki testing offers a practical and testable rationale — that lives spent preying upon others, lives of spite, cynicism, and hatred, are weaker than lives of cooperation, teamwork, kindness, blessing, and joy.

Hate another and it is you who are damaged. Bless another and it is you who are blessed and healed.

See for yourself.

Books, Movies and Videos

Books, Movies and Videos

Books

The following is a sample list of books (and other resources) that I have found particularly useful and meaningful, or that have been strongly recommended by others.

Aikido Journal, Aiki News, 50-B Peninsula Center Dr. #317, Rolling Hills Estates, CA 90724. Phone/Fax: (310) 265-0351

Aikido Today Magazine, Areté Press, P.O. Box #1060, Claremont, CA 91711-1060. Phone: (909) 624-7770, FAX: (800) 445-AIKI E-mail: atm@aiki.com   Website: http://www.aiki.com/ATM

History, culture, and practice in the world of Aikido. Interviews with Aikidoists, beginning and advanced, from around the country and the world; calendars of events, announcements, reviews of books, training tapes, and other products.

Conari Press (1993), *Random Acts of Kindness*: Conari Press, Berkeley, CA, 160 p.

A wonderful collection of *entoku*, "good done in secret." Notice how often accounts appear of kindnesses done in traffic, how important and remarkable these small kindnesses were to the recipients. If nothing else, read the foreword by D. R. Kingma — then go and do likewise.

Covey, Stephen R. (1989), *The 7 Habits of Highly Effective People — Restoring the Character Ethic*: Simon & Schuster, NY, 358 p.

___ (1995), *Living the 7 Habits:* Simon & Schuster audiotape.

Ki instructors talk about "living positively." Here's the laboratory manual or user guide on *how* to do it. Audiotapes narrated by the author are available excerpting this best-selling book. The subtitle refers to Covey's survey of 200 years of American "success literature." That written during the first hundred years of this country was based upon character and ethics — integrity, honesty, reliability. He found success literature written during the past 50 years to be quite different.

Crum, Thomas F. (1987), *The Magic of Conflict*: Simon & Schuster, Inc., NY, 256 p.

Conflict from a most unusual point of view — not as a negative to be overcome, but as a positive and active opportunity for creation. Includes a tale of Koichi Tohei, student of Morihei Ueshiba (founder of Aikido). Suppose you had been following the Way of Harmony but now it is World War II and you find yourself as commanding officer of Japanese troops charged with invasion of China. What would you do? Here is Tohei's solution to that dilemma.

Dobson, Terry, and Miller, Victor (1987), *Aikido in Everyday Life — Giving in to Get Your Way:* North Atlantic Books, Berkeley, CA, 256 p.

Could easily be subtitled: "Suzette Elgin Meets Morihei Ueshiba." Aikido *off* the mat and dealing with conflict and harmony in, yes, the most everyday events of everyday life, from breakfast to boardroom to PTA and bedtime for the kids. Translates aggression and defense into the visible realm through the geometry of triangle, circle, square. A Hard Truth: because most attacks and assaults are non-physical, using physical responses (throws and blows to the overbearing boss or annoying co-worker) are in the realm of fantasy. Here's how to deal with real life. See Elgin, Suzette for superb treatment of "verbal assault." See the movie *Grand Canyon* for an outstanding example of the triangle, circle, square defense (see *Movies and Videos*).

The first edition of this book was published in 1977 when *Winning Through Intimidation* and *Taking Care of Number One* topped the best-seller lists. "The art of Aikido was virtually unknown outside of Japan," noted Dobson, "and the idea that precepts deriving from a martial art (much less a martial art devoted to peace) could illuminate the conduct of one's daily affairs was too radical a notion for most publishers to consider seriously. Add to that Aikido's insistence on responsibility for the protection of one's adversary and it seems an absolute miracle the book got published when it did." Invaluable. For insights on the late great Terry Dobson himself, see Heckler (1985).

Ebert, Roger (1994), *Ebert's Little Movie Glossary — A Compendium of Movie Clichés, Stereotypes, Obligatory Scenes, Hackneyed Formulas, Shopworn Conventions, and Outdated Archetypes:* Andrews and McMeel, MO, 116 p.

Do you or your children believe what you see on TV or in the movies? Here's the hilarious antidote. Also on CompuServe: GO MOVIES. Select "Roger Ebert's movie reviews." Click the Movie Center button then select "Glossary of Movie Terms."

Elgin, Suzette Haden (1989), *Success with the Gentle Art of Verbal Self-Defense*: Prentice Hall, NJ, 288 p.

___(1987), *The Last Word on the Gentle Art of Verbal Self-Defense*: Prentice Hall, NJ, 246 p.

___(1980), *The Gentle Art of Verbal Self-Defense*: Prentice Hall, NJ, 310 p.

On the mat we learn to recognize a physical attack for what it is and respond appropriately. Here is Aikido applied to verbal and emotional attacks which are far more common than mere *physical* attack and far more difficult to deal with as training is so rare. The phrase "on the street" as commonly heard and interpreted in martial arts classes is usually nonsense — the real battlegrounds are in the shop, the office, the boardroom, the kitchen, the bedroom, the bar, the beltway. The weapons are words and their underlying attitudes, against which physical techniques are wildly inappropriate or impossible.

Elgin provides rare and valuable training in the tools and the ethics of their use. Compare the linguistic concept of "matching Satir modes" with the Aikido concept of matching speed and direction, blending with the partner or attacker before actual execution of a technique. There are more books in this series, all excellent and uniquely valuable. She talks Virginia Satir and family relationships but you may hear Lady Jessica and the Bene Gesserit training from Frank Herbert's *Dune* (book— *not* movie). See also Dobson, 1987.

Fazzioli, E. (1986), *Chinese Calligraphy*: Abbeville Press, NY, 252 p.

A delightful and informative text for anyone wishing to understand more about Chinese ideograms (the source of Japanese *kanji* such as the *ki*, *qi*, or *chi* symbol), their history and development.

Frankl, Viktor (1984*), Man's Search for Meaning — An Introduction to Logotherapy*: Simon & Schuster, NY, 189 p.

The definitive treatise on changing one's point of view. The idea of changing one's point of view to "Thank you for the opportunity to practice my Aikido" is extremely frightening to some. "That's impossible!" cried one student — and left. It is quite possible. Psychologist Viktor Frankl did it in a Nazi concentration camp.

"We who lived in concentration camps can remember the men who walked through the huts comforting others, giving away their last piece of bread. They may have been few in number, but they offer

sufficient proof that everything can be taken away from a man but one thing: the last of the human freedoms — to choose one's attitude in any given set of circumstances, to choose one's own way."

Fritz, Robert (1989), *The Path of Least Resistance*: Fawcett Columbine, NY, 286 p.

On becoming the creative force in your own life. Why tackling a problem with grim determination and willpower may not be the best solution. There is a newer edition; this one is more terse.

Fulghum, Robert (1988), *All I Really Need to Know I Learned in Kindergarten*: Villard Books, NY, 196 p.

If you are having trouble making your list of things "good, or true, or beautiful," they're all here, from universal spirit and doing good in secret, to the 145th reincarnation of the Haiho Lama into the body of shoemaker Elias Schwartz through an error in the cosmic switching yards. Excerpted on audio tape.

___ (1989), *It Was On Fire When I Lay Down On It*: Villard Books, NY, 218 p.

More of the above but even better. The story of Alexander Papaderos, the man with a mirror and an answer to the eternal question "What is the Meaning of Life?" is especially wise and beautiful.

Gluck, Jay (1996), *Zen Combat — and the Secret Power Called Ki*: Personally Oriented, Ashiya, Japan, and Weatherhill, NY, 288 p.

A new edition of a wonderful classic. Gluck's 1957 *True* magazine article essentially introduced karate to America. "Modern Zen Fools" is the encounter between Morihei Ueshiba and cartoonist/engineer Rube Goldberg. Priceless for charm, wit, and history of martial arts.

Heckler, Richard Strozzi (Ed.) (1985), *Aikido and the New Warrior*: North Atlantic Books, Berkeley, CA.

A treasury of essays on Aikido, including the late Terry Dobson's wrenching short story about "real Aikido." In "A Kind Word Turneth Away Wrath" he tells of leaving the train feeling ashamed and humbled. I felt ashamed and humbled just reading the story. Terry describes his then-self as an "arrogant jock." Those who studied with him later report that the constant refrain of this immensely strong, powerful man was "Gently! Softly!" See also Dobson (1987).

— (1984), *The Anatomy of Change — East/West Approaches to Body/Mind Therapy*: Shambhala Publications, Boston, MA, 138 p.

Essays on Aikido applied to all facets of daily life. Again, practice on the mat is only one small part.

Hyams, Joe (1982), *Zen in the Martial Arts*: Bantam Books, Inc., NY, 134 p.

Essays on fundamentals of the martial arts and *budo* — a Lessons-Learned Report by a student of the late Bruce Lee. Ueshiba was rooted in Shinto which shares common threads with Buddhism, Christianity, and the teachings of the old yogis. The Great Truths are universal.

Heyerdahl, Thor (1989) *Easter Island — The Mystery Solved*: Random House, NY, 10022, 256 p.

A profusely illustrated summary of Heyerdahl's investigations on Easter Island including the 1986 demonstration of a 30-ton statue "walking" thanks to basic physics — and One-Point.

Internet Addresses and Resources for Aikido — a Brief List

See Kjartan Clausen's excellent Aikido FAQ list. One of the most comprehensive Aikido information resources on the Internet.

http://www.ii.uib.no/~kjartan/aikidofaq

For Japanese language glossary, current Aikido-L subscription information (and unsubscribing), see Jun Akiyama's webpage at:

http://www.aikiweb.com

The Official Ki Society Web Page strives for updated Ki Society dojo addresses and information.

http://pw1.netcom.com/~aikidoki/Directory.html

The "Unofficial Ki Society Web Page" includes essays, commentary:

http://www.unofficial.ki-society.org

The Virginia Ki Society offers training notes, books, and other materials: http://vakisociety.org

An Aikido calendar, suppliers, publications, organizations, and links:

http://www-cse.ucsd.edu/users/paloma/Aikido/aikido_info.html

For a very different point of view, a conservative warning site is at:

http://www.iclnet.org/pub/resources/text/cri/cri-jrnl/crj0167a.txt

Lewis, C. S. (1982), *The Screwtape Letters*: Macmillan Publishing Co., Inc., NY, 172 p.

Advice from a Senior Devil to a Junior Temptor on capturing human souls. This classic gem provides a different premise and point of view (about 180 degrees) off the norm. Here, the usually garrulous C. S. Lewis is relatively terse and to-the-point. In Aikido, beginners typically spend about six months or so huddling together over after-class beers debating whether or not *ki* is "real." If you're having this problem, see letters I and XXX for a pungent review of the peculiar human concept of "reality."

Maruyama, Koretoshi (1984), *Aikido With Ki* : Ki No Kenkyukai, Tokyo, 208 p. [Distributor: Harper & Row, Inc., NY.]

The Virginia Ki Society uses this "Green Book" as its official text. If there is any question on how to do a technique (the physical and the *ki*), check this source.

Millman, Dan (1984), *The Way of the Peaceful Warrior*: H. J. Kramer, Tiburon, CA, 210 p.

Whether it is fact or fiction is irrelevant; it has insights.

Peck, M. Scott (1983), *People of the Lie — The Hope for Healing Human Evil*: Simon and Schuster, NY, 272 p.

A best-seller that many bought but few have read. I know of many people and groups who set out to read it but "couldn't get through it" because it was "too disturbing." It is indeed a disturbing, a treatise on the existence, nature, and properties of Evil. A current popular notion is that Evil does not exist, in part, a problem of terminology. Peck provides an invaluable working psychological definition: Evil is "that which seeks to kill life or liveliness." It is the opposite of Good, "that which promotes life and liveliness."

— (1978), *The Road Less Traveled — A New Psychology of Love, Traditional Values, and Spiritual Growth*: Simon and Schuster, NY, 316 p.

Love and *pacifism* have both suffered strange perversions of meaning in our society. For a discussion of true kindness and love, Dr. Peck's chapters on what love *is* and what love *is not* are unequaled. These alone are worth the price of the book which has been on a best-seller list at some time during every year since it was first published. Read this, then see Saotome (1993). These two books are the antidote to the parallel delusions of *love* as "warm fuzzy feeling" or "doormat," and to *pacifism* as "doormat" or "dead."

Pipher, Mary (1994), *Reviving Ophelia — Saving the Selves of Adolescent Girls*: Ballantine Books, NY, 304 p.

A gritty look at the very real consequences of our media-soaked society, what our glorification of sex and violence is doing to our children, and case histories of those who are paying the consequences. Pipher calls for a "new form of self-defense" and offers a new definition of freedom. *Freedom* is not the liberty to blow here and there with the voices of parents, friends, the media, or the winds of the day. *Freedom* is effective setting of goals and "sailing toward your dreams." The author is also remarkable for the ability to appreciate a client for who and what she is at the time, then build on that. Perhaps all counselors are trained to do so, but here it is striking.

Reed, William (1986), *Ki — A Practical Guide for Westerners*: Japan Publications, Inc., NY, 226 p.

Ki is a foreign concept to many Americans. Reed uses familiar terms and a wealth of example and commentary to explain Japanese traditions including *ki* principles and exercises, the tea ceremony, calligraphy, and *Noh* drama, and their relationship to Aikido and the martial arts.

See Reed's comments on the use of the Noh mask; compare with the scene in *Star Wars* in which Luke first meets Princess Leia. Although he is disguised in the Imperial uniform and helmet, Leia remarks that he doesn't look like a stormtrooper — why? Notice his expressive use of the mask.

___(1992), *Ki — A Road That Anyone Can Walk*: Japan Publications, Inc., NY, 340 p.

From the history of Koichi Tohei and Ki Society International, to *ki* in business and daily life. Includes commentary on philosophy, healing, and daily disciplines.

There is also a delightful selection of Japanese- and Chinese-style poetry (some intended to be chanted to folk tunes while training with a staff), and a collection of *Ki* Sayings from Master Tohei, here presented in English translation for the first time.

Saotome, Mitsugi (1993), *Aikido and the Harmony of Nature*: Shambhala Publications, Inc., Boston, MA, 252 p.

Contains history and anecdotes of Aikido founder Morihei Ueshiba; Saotome was one of his live-in students (*uchi-deshi*). Ranges from the ideals of honor and service in the *samurai* tradition, to the elements of "reality," wave-forms, gravity, and spirituality. These concepts are woven into the descriptions of individual Aikido techniques. Excellent.

___ (1989), *The Principles of Aikido*: Shambhala Publications, Inc., Boston, MA, 224 p.

Aikido philosophy and techniques. Particularly remarkable for the chapters on "The Sword" and "Ukemi." If you are caught in the common delusion of *nage* as "winner" and *uke* as "loser," this will help you see *ukemi* (giving attacks and taking falls) as discipline and art in its own right.

Stone, John and Meyer, Ron, Eds. (1989), *Aikido in America*: Frog, Ltd., P.O. Box 12327, Berkeley, CA, 330 p.

Interviews with two generations of American Aikidoists: Terry Dobson to George Simcox. A wonderful collection of observations by those who studied under or observed *O-Sensei* in action.

Swett, Ben H. (1997), *Inner Life Laboratory*: Round Earth Publishing, Merrifield, VA 22116-3855.

A "laboratory manual" for the soul. Exercises in point of view, in wise kindness, in power and purpose. Some exerpts available at the following address: http:\\www.xis.com\~bhs\spirit.html.

Stevens, John (1984), Aikido — The Way of Harmony: Shambhala Publications, Boston, MA,198 p.

Contains biographies of the Founder of Aikido, Morihei Ueshiba, and of Shirata Rinjiro, the author's instructor. Detailed analysis of Aikido techniques including such basics as proper bowing, sitting, standing, breathing. *Hambu*-style terms are slightly different from those used in the style of *Shin-Shin-Toitsu Aikido*. Extensive photographs.

Thich Nhat Hanh (Mobi Ho, Trans.) (1987), *The Miracle of Mindfulness — A Manual on Meditation*: Beacon Press, Boston, MA,140 p.

On becoming aware. This man and his followers were persecuted in their native Viet Nam because they insisted on tending the wounded, suffering, and dying — regardless of which side they had fought on.

In "Random Acts of Kindness" (see Conari Press, 1993) there is a haunting story told by an American who was wounded during an attack on a Vietnamese village. As he lay helpless in his blood, an old woman approached and gave him — not the final blow he expected but — a cup of tea. Then she quietly went her way.

Tohei, Koichi (1983), *Kiatsu*: Ki No Kenkyukai H.Q., Tokyo, Japan [Kodansha International/USA, Ltd, through Harper & Row, Publishers, Inc., NY], 180 p.

Kiatzu techniques, the application of *ki* to healing. Descriptions and explanations of the *Ki* Exercises for Health and other warm-up exercises begin on page 120.

— (1978), *Ki in Daily Life*: Ki No Kenkyukai H.Q., Tokyo, Japan, 136 p.

I was pleased to have read this book just for the commentary on the Japanese phrase *suisei-mushi*, meaning "to be born drunk and to die while still dreaming" (see page 15).

Koichi Tohei, student and *uchi-deshi* of Aikido founder Morihei Ueshiba, is the founder of *Shin-shin Toitsu Aikido*, the style of Aikido practiced by the Virginia Ki Society.

— (1976), *Book of Ki — Coordinating Mind and Body in Daily Life*: Japan Publications, Inc., NY, 102 p.

From training body, mind, and soul to raising a golf handicap. Contains exercises and an introduction to *kiatzu*, a method of healing with *ki*.

Ueshiba, Kisshomaru (1987), *The Spirit of Aikido*: Kodansha International, Tokyo, Japan,126 p.

Kisshomaru Ueshiba is the son of Morihei Ueshiba, Founder of Aikido, and the head of Aikikai. Presents a detailed review of the underlying philosophy of Aikido and its pre-WWII history.

Westbrook, A., and Ratti, O. (1970), *Aikido and the Dynamic Sphere — An Illustrated Introduction*: Charles E. Tuttle Company, Rutland, VT, 376 p.

I first saw this book in a martial arts supply store where I had gone to purchase a wooden practice sword. Near the door was a wide selection of video tapes, featuring snarling bloody actors and titles such as *The Art of Killing*. A mannikin in black *ninja* uniform, armed to the teeth, stood by a poster advertising classes in the "secrets of Japan's professional assassins." The counter at back held throwing stars, daggers, spikes, steel claws, and a warning that these could not be sold to anyone under 18 without parental permission. The store clerks themselves didn't look that old. I found the only book on Aikido in the entire store, and opening it at random, found this line: *"If you harm your opponent unnecessarily, you have failed."* It's an excellent book, but on that day I would have bought it just for that.

This is *the* textbook on Aikido, so widely used that in 1994 it was in its 42nd printing; in 1984 I bought the 27th printing. Besides an extensive essay on the ethics of martial arts, the authors delve into every aspect of the art. Sections address such topics as "Immobilization no. 1 against attack no. 3" but the Japanese names that we use are supplied in the glossary. Reading it is difficult for a beginner; it was two years before the technique instructions made sense to me, partly because of differences between *Hambu* style and Ki Society style and terms.

It is invaluable for the superb line-drawings which emphasize the circular motions. These drawings enjoy the dubious honor of being the most-plagiarized illustrations in the history of martial arts. If you have seen a beautiful, flowing line drawing of an Aikido throw or *jo-kata* on a poster or advertisement, chances are excellent that it came from this book. Buy it for the equally valuable text.

Zi, Nancy (1986), *The Art of Breathing*: Bantam Books, 158 p.

Thirty exercises (with visualizations) for improved breathing. In Aikido, as in yoga and other arts, breathing is a discipline in and of itself. The idea is this: If you can't control your own breathing, you control nothing.

Movies and Videos

Lists of movies and videos related to Aikido or *ki* tend to emphasize the Japanese *samurai* tradition. Yet many martial arts movies emphasize physical skills but lack values or preach those of the worst possible kind. Here are more mainstream American works which would not, at first glance, be associated with Aikido or martial arts, but which demonstrate Aikido principles if only in a few key scenes.

The internal principles of Aikido are not limited to certain geographic settings, equipment, plots, or actors. They are universal. If they are to be developed at all they must be observed, considered, practiced, and developed in daily life.

While most movies and videos here are fictional, the ideas behind them and the people who choose to convey these particular ideas are quite real.[16] Observe the underlying purpose and intent.

Bad Day at Black Rock

Classic tale by John Sturges, director of *The Great Escape* and *The Magnificent Seven*. By merely appearing unannounced and unexpected, a mild-mannered stranger (Spencer Tracey) sends a small town with a dark secret into a frenzy of suspicion and fear. A story of choices: the shame and guilt of having made the wrong ones, the terror and opportunity of a second chance. Includes a short scene of karate versus the classic Western bully filmed in 1954 when karate was still a rare and exotic oriental art.

Clean and Sober

Facing drug and murder charges, real-estate hotshot Daryl Poynter (Michael Keaton) decides that a drug clinic, with its guarantee of complete anonymity, would be the perfect hideout — and is in for a big surprise. While this appears to be a movie drug addiction, it is actually about *addiction* in its endless variety, whether to external sources or

---

[16] Beginners often ask: "Who's your favorite martial artist?" Mine is a retired Air Force colonel, but what they usually mean is "which movie star?" Well, OK, Colonel Potter of "M.A.S.H." I've learned a lot from that fictional character and the writers who created him. Most "martial arts" characters can kick and punch, but neither they nor the producers behind them seem to have a clue as to how to live or the consequences involved once the fight scene is over and the money has been collected.

internal ones, whether material goods, alcohol, sex, food, self-image or the desire to prey on or to control others to hide one's own lack of self-control. Consider the different images of car headlights presented at the beginning of the film and at the very end. Morgan Freeman as a drug counselor and M. Emmet Walsh as an Alcoholics Anonymous counselor can't be fooled because they've been there themselves and already know all the lies.

The Firm

One of the few modern movies, including martial arts and others, where the protagonist uses his head rather than just punching or running. A mysterious law firm spins a web of easy money and material things. No one has ever escaped and lived until neophyte lawyer Mitch McDeere (Tom Cruise) finds a way out with a small but powerful weapon of the law and negotiation. The FBI investigator, wanting something a bit more dramatic is incredulous, yet "it's more than you had on Al Capone," points out McDeere. Dramatic and bombastic not necessary — just what works. An excellent performance by Gene Hackman as a lonely man who wishes he had done better — and does.

Grand Canyon

A strange and beautiful look at violence, real and imaginary, the interrelationships between lives and the things that actually matter. In the beginning moments of this film you will see a great Aikido Master working as a towtruck driver (Danny Glover). Watch what he does and how he does it then compare his actions with Terry Dobson's diagrams for attack and defense. (See Dobson, 1987.) Another haunting scene is Steve Martin's portrayal of a movie maker exploiting the lucrative genre of make-believe violence; after a real mugging he sees the light — then chooses to walk back into the darkness.

The Great Escape

Based on a true story of Allied prisoners of war who tunnelled out of a German prison camp. Of the 75 escapees, those who got into gun battles at the rail stations, punched out guards, stole bombers and other dramatic and highly visible solutions to the problem, never made it. This is the source of the famous scene (and poster) of Steve McQueen fruitlessly attempting to elude Nazi pursuers via motorcycle stunts. (Legend has it that he refused to make the movie unless allowed to film this bravura sequence.)

Who actually escaped? Only three: two who posed as harmless fishermen and one on a bicycle, all with a firm goal but who moved so calmly and gently that they never aroused the suspicions of watching soldiers. Also notice the character and behavior of the camp commandant and those under his command in contrast to more modern portrayals of German troops. See *Schindler's List.*

Groundhog Day

A charming remake of the legend of the Flying Dutchman of folklore with a kinder, gentler, wiser ending. The profoundly unlovable and unloving Bill Murray is trapped within the same day, apparently doomed to live it over and over — forever. What would you do if you could live forever? What would you do if no one knew? How long before money, manipulation, and preying on others becomes very very boring? What counts? What's next?

Hidden Fortress

George Lucas' 1977 movie "Star Wars" is the most popular American movie ever made. This 1958 Japanese film by Akira Kurosawa was the inspiration. Lucas saw it in film school and never forgot it. Toshiro Mifune is general Rokurota Makabe, who in "Star Wars" becomes Obi-wan Kenobi, Princess Yukihime becomes Princess Leia Organa, and the two hapless wandering foot soldiers who come to the rescue of the disguised princess become C3PO and R2D2. The Source of the Force.

Police Academy 6

See "Soundman's" battle with a bad guy. OK, it's the Keystone Cops and it's a cartoon, but consider the idea of "Thank you for the opportunity to practice my Aikido" with a slightly different emphasis: "Thank you for the opportunity to practice my sound effects." Either way, the emphasis is *not* on the attacker.

Powers of Ten

A breathtaking change in point of view. A man dozes on a picnic blanket in lake-side Chicago. Every ten seconds we are ten times further out from our starting point until our galaxy is only a distant glimmer of light. The viewpoint then returns to the man's hand at the rate of 10 times more magnification every ten seconds, ending within a proton of a carbon atom. The Films of Charles & Ray Eames, Volume 1. The video is $39.95 from Pyramid Film & Video, 2801 Colorado Avenue, Santa Monica, CA 90404, 1-(800) 421-2304.

Royal Wedding

Thin plot, but the source of the famous scene in which Fred Astair dances with a hatrack. As always he makes his partner look very very good. No clash. Only blending and flowing. Consider this in dealing with *uke*.

Schindler's List

Nazis and World War II German soldiers are the all-purpose bad guys, the monsters we love to hate. Our memories revolve around the innocents destroyed by gas and guns. Forgotten are the other casualties, the soldiers themselves, many forced or deceived into taking part in a great wrong. In a final scene of this powerful movie, news is received that Germany has surrendered. The war is over, but now the *Schindlerjuden* face the prospect of being shot down in mass by their former guards.

Schindler saves not only his workers but the soldiers too, by presenting them with what may have been their first real choice in many years — to give in to the temptation of murder and vengeance and the destruction of their own souls, or, to simply stop, to return to their homes with clean hands, as men, not as murderers.

> *"Behold!" says God.*
> *"I have set before you the way of Good and the way of Evil.*
> *The way of Life and the way of Death.*
> *Choose Life!"*

The Shawshank Redemption

To redeem is defined in part as: "To recover ownership of something through payment of a sum, to fulfill a pledge, to set free, rescue or ransom."

A financial planner (Tim Robbins) is wrongly condemned for life to Shawshank Prison for murdering his wife. The experienced inmates bet that this quiet man will crack the first night. Not only does he not crack, ever, but in the course of a secret 20-year goal he starts a library, an education program, and groundwork to rescue the prison from the control of a sadistic warden. Red (Morgan Freeman) on his way to die, keeps a pledge that enables his friend to save his life, enables Red to choose life.

While this movie appears at first to be about surviving the rigors of prison, it is actually about goals, and soft, gentle, persistent progress towards those goals, blooming where you're planted, and life — any life — as an act of creation.

The Seven Samurai

Most wars have been fought over who gets to keep the food the farmers grow. In Greco-Roman mythology, Mars, the god of war, was originally a god of agriculture. This practical need to protect the crops is also the root of the Japanese *samurai* and of martial arts from other lands. (Note that *numchuks*, which we know only as a martial arts weapon, are actually a farm tool, a flail, for threshing rice).

In this classic film by Akira Kurosawa a village hires seven *samurai* (with a youthful Toshiro Mifune as a would-be *samurai*) for protection against the annual harvest-time raiders. In the test set by the village headman for selecting candidates, observe who wins and why.

(This movie inspired Hollywood's "Magnificent Seven" cast as a western; director John Sturges seems to have carefully matched the faces and personalities of the original Japanese actors).

Side Kicks

An asthmatic youth lost in a fantasy world is taken in hand by the canny and kindly Mr. Lee (Mako) who leads him out of the trap of fantasy into the world of real competence, true confidence, and genuine self-control. All the elements of the standard martial arts movie are here: good guy, bad guy, the opportunity to "take revenge" on one's opponent by beating him to a pulp — and they are all slyly lampooned and redirected.

The enemy is not really the class bully; it is asthma. The karate competition is won not by trashing an adversary but by "breaking," an exercise in concentration and self-control. The beautiful girl is not the prize won by defeat of a rival; she already liked him anyway — for himself. And "don't need karate *gi*," points out Mr. Lee (who races from kitchen to competition in an apron) "to break blocks."

Chuck Norris' all-time best movie pokes gentle fun at all his others. While it suggests the value of hero-worship for setting direction and goals (the boy in the final scene gave me goosebumps), emphasis is firmly placed on the need to move beyond.

The Star Wars Trilogy

Star Wars: Many of the concepts attributed to "The Force" come directly from Aikido. Darth Vader's hissing breath is a wonderful parody of *ki* breathing and his helmet is the traditional *samurai* helmet and bamboo armor reinterpreted in black plastic. (See the movie *Teenage Mutant Ninja Turtles* for an example of the almost-real thing worn by the wicked Shredder.) Observe Ben Kenobi's calm and impartial graciousness to all, even the despised 'droids, in contrast to the generally spiteful and frenetic behavior of almost all other main characters. (This same character of calm graciousness is displayed by Master Splinter, the *ninja* rat in *Teenage Mutant Ninja Turtles*.)

An Aikido joke in circulation since this 1977 movie is that "The Force" — one side light, one side dark, that "binds the universe together" — actually refers to duct tape.

The Empire Strikes Back: Who has Luke destroyed when he strikes down his enemy in the cave? The inspiration for Yoda is believed to be Misao Shoji of Gardena, California. A superb Aikidoist, he is also renowned for his pixilated sense of humor. His favorite song, "Found A Peanut," is sure to be sung several times in the course of any workshop where he is present.

Return of the Jedi: *On video and in slow motion*, watch the clash between Vader and Emperor. Someone went to great effort to compose scenes invisible at normal film speed, not seen in the theatre. Compare with Saotome's (1993) account of experience as Ueshiba's *uke*.

Star Wars comes directly from *The Hidden Fortress* by Akira Kurosawa (also the source of *The Seven Samurai* which became Hollywood's *The Magnificent Seven*). George Lucas told Kurosawa that he saw *The Hidden Fortress* in film school and never forgot it.

Weapons of the Spirit

A documentary of a little French town of pacifist Huguenots that spent the years of World War II rescuing fugitive Jews. We hear and dwell much on the perversion of good by evil; here is a stunning example of the perversion of evil by good. Written and directed by Pierre Sauvage who was born in the town during his parents' sojourn there.

Index

Index

—A—

Addiction, 195, 166, 195
Ahimsa, 176
Aiki, 4
Aikido, definition, 1
Alpha waves, 151
Anecdotes
  A Positive Boss, 169
  Cigars and CBS, 166
  Dave Butts, defensive tackle, 5
  Dick ("The Bruiser") Addis and
    Unliftable Body, 118
  Golden Gloves, 80
  Heaven and Hell, 111
  Karate Blocks and Ikkyo, 132
  Laughing *Uke*, 169
  Monkey Trap, 81
  One Thousand Rolls, 29
  Resisting Arrest, 68
  The Empty Boat, 157
  The Invisible *Tenkan*, 34
  The Marching Men, 44
  The Policeman's Tale, 175
  Ueshiba's Swordless Duel, 2
  Unbendable Semantics, 50
  War of the Worlds, 165
  WWII Wallpaper, 174
Animals, kindness to, 177
Astair, Fred, and hatrack, 198
Asthma, 145

—B—

Bonsai, 146
Breaking blocks, 107
Breathing, incorrect and
  symptoms, 141
Buddha, 11
Budo, 55, 182
  Defined, 2
  traditions, 3

—C—

Center of gravity, 8
Competition, 2, 155
Cross rolls, 30
Cross-legged sitting, 23
Cynicism, 168

—D—

Discernment, 172
Dobson, Terry, 173, 188, 192
Duct tape and The Force, 200

—E—

Easter Island and One-Point, 44
Einstein, Albert, 6
Entoku, 177, 185
Eyes and attention, 137

—F—

Feeling vs. seeing, 77
Force, The, 197, 200
Ford, Henry, 12

—G—

Giving, effect on others, 175
Gluck, Jay, 163, 188
Goals, 191, 199
Goldberg, Rube, 163
Good and Evil, 126, 172, 176,
  190, 198, 200
Good done in secret, 177, 185
Graciousness, 200

—H—

Hakama Effect, 67
Hakama Toe, 126

Hanmi, 32
Happo-undo, 135
Hara, 8, 43
Hypnosis, 12

—I—

Ikkyo, 105
Ikkyo-undo, 131, 133
Impartiality, 176, 200
Integrity, 185
Integrity and impartiality, 176

—J—

Jesus, 6, 126, 164

—K—

Karate stances, 32
Katsu jin ken, 3
Kendall, Steve, 170
Ki, 1, 10, 11
Ki testing, 3
Ki testing, reason for, 10
ki, defined, 4
Koho-tento-undo, 25
Kurosawa, Akira, 197, 200

—L—

Lee, Rev. Gerald Stanley, 34
Leverage, 138

—M—

Ma-ai, 156
Magnetic Hand, 37, 39
Mars, god of war, 199
Martial artist, favorite, 195
Master Splinter, 200
Meaning of Life, 188
Media, 165
Movie monsters, 138
Mudra, 159

—N—

Navratilova, Martina, 173
Noble Warrior, 182
Nonaka, Takashi, 5
Numchuks, 199

—O—

"On the street", 24, 155, 165
One-Man Taigi, 170
O-Sensei. See Ueshiba, Morihei

—P—

Physics, 7, 85, 87, 97, 105, 138,
    154
Pneuma, 4
Point of view, 46, 91, 146, 164,
    169, 174, 175, 187, 197
Prayer, 114, 181

—Q—

Quotations
    Buchanan, D. C., 76
    Buddha, 11
    Chandler, Susan, 123
    Ford, Henry, 12
    Freud, Sigmund, 4
    Gluck, Jay, 163
    Jesus, 4, 176
    Navratilova, Martina, 173
    Nonaka, Takashi, 5
    Saotome, Mitsugi, 2
    Simcox, George, 24, 53, 73, 75,
        80, 101, 118, 162, 167
    St. Paul of Tarsus, 164
    St. Theresa of Lisieux, 171
    Swett, Ben, 13, 142, 167
    Tohei, Koichi, 106, 143, 155,
        171
    Ueshiba, Morihei, 2, 55, 126,
        171
    Welles, Orson, 165

—R—

Reality, 6, 168, 190
Reality testing, 14
Reed, Will, 2, 191
Reigi, defined, 72
Relaxation, defined, 65
Revenge, 166, 173, 199
Rolling, 24
Rolling, backwards, 27, 31
Rolling, forward, 28
Rolling, tumbling rolls, 29
Rolls, Cross, 30
Ruach, 4

—S—

Samurai, 2
Saotome, Mitsugi, 2, 200
Seiza stool, 21
Seiza, defined, 21
Shain, Merle, 175
Shin-Shin Toitsu Aikido, 3, 10
Shoji, Misao, 200
Shomen-uchi, 107
Simcox, George, v, 24, 75, 80,
     101, 118, 162, 167, 192
Sitting, *seiza,* 21
Sitting, cross-legged, 23
Skating, One-Point in, 43
Spiritual Spectrum, 4, 172, 176,
     177
Standing, *hanmi*, 32
Strength vs. tension, 20
Supernatural powers, 13
Swett, Ben, 142, 167

—T—

Talmud, 177
Tan-t'ien, 43
Tekubi-shindo undo, 62

Tenkan, 34
Tohei, Koichi, v, 3, 106, 143, 152,
     155, 171, 186
Traffic, 155, 185
Turning, 34
Turning the other cheek, 3, 34,
     126
TV and radio, 165, 191

—U—

Ude-furi choyaku undo, 70
Ude-furi undo, 70
Udemawashi-undo, 87
Ueshiba, Morihei, 1, 2, 55, 66,
     126, 151, 163, 171, 182, 192
Unbendable Arm, 18, 40

—V—

Vader, Darth, 200
Verbal Self-Defense, 186,187

—W—

War of the Worlds, 165
Welles, Orson, 165
Wesley, John, 151
Win-lose, 169, 170
Wordsworth, William, 177
World War II, 2, 174, 186, 198,
     200

—Y—

Yoda, 200

—Z—

Zempo-kaiten waza, 30
Zengo-undo, 134, 135

Afterword

We hope you have found this *Sampler* useful and helpful.

If you have corrections or comments, or if you have an exercise or illustrative anecdote that you would like to share for possible inclusion in future editions, please write me at:

> Round Earth Publishing
> P.O. Box 3855
> Dept. 150
> Merrifield, VA 22116

> E-mail: 71021.744@CompuServe.com

All additions will be gratefully acknowledged.

C. M. Shifflett

Appendix A.
Ki Society Dojos

Appendix A. Ki Society Dojos

The following is a list of schools of *ki* and *Ki-Aikido*. Those in bold type and starred are operated by Chief Instructors recognized by the *Ki* Society International in Tokyo, Japan. Most have additional educational or outreach programs at other locations. Call or write for information. Note that some addresses below are points of information rather than the address of the dojo itself. Please send corrections to The Official Ki Society Web Page at:

http://pw1.netcom.com/~aikidoki
e-mail: intoku@aol.com

or to:
Round Earth Publishing,
P.O. Box 3855, Merrifield, VA 22116
71021.744@CompuServe.com

Japan
Ki Society World Headquarters/Ki no Sato*
Ki no Kenkyukai So-Honbu
3515 O-aza Akabane
Ichikai-machi, Haga-gun
Tochigi-ken
Phone: 0285-68-4000

Ki Society Tokyo Headquarters*
Ki no Kenkyukai Tokyo Chiku Honbu
101 Ushigome Heim
2-30 Haramachi, Shinjuku-ku
Tokyo 162
Phone: 03-3353-3461
FAX: 03-3353-1897

USA
Arizona

Arizona Ki Society*
P. O. Box 13285
Scottsdale, AZ 85267
Attn: Kirk Fowler
Phone: (602) 991-6467
kfowler@aol.com
Dojo:
7845 E. Evans Road, Suite F
Scottsdale, AZ 85260
Phone: (602) 991-6467
Aikidorat@aol.com or dratynsk@aol.com

California

Northern California Ki Society*
2414 Sixth Street
Berkeley, CA 94710
Attn: Pietro Yuji Maida
Phone: (510) 848-3437
FAX: (510) 848-1327
intoku@aol.com
http://Socrates.berkeley.edu/~cdea/JCAC.html

Southern California Ki Society*
P. O. Box 3752
Gardena, CA 90247
Attn: Clarence Chinn
Phone: (310) 370-1956

**Southern California Ki Society
 Santa Barbara***
255 Magnolia
Goleta, CA 93117
Attn: Steve Ota
Phone: (805) 967-3101
FAX: (805) 967-5459

Colorado

Rocky Mountain Ki Society
P. O. Box 11191
Denver, CO 80211
Attn: Russell Jones
Phone: (303) 425-0988

Hawaii

Big Island Aikido-Ki Society*
P. O. Box 438
Papaikou, HI 96781-0438
Attn: Takashi Nonaka, Roy Yonemori
Phone: (808) 964-1480

Honolulu Ki Society*
2003 Nuuanu Avenue
Honolulu, HI 96817-2502
Phone: (808) 373-1864
Attn: Seichi Tabata, Byron Nakamura

Kauai Ki Society*
Box 506
Eleele, HI 96705-0506
Attn: Richard Kuboyama, Lloyd Miyashiro
Phone: (808) 335-5387

Aloha Ki Society
60 N. Kuakini St., 4-C
Honolulu, HI 96817
Attn: Harry Eto, Don Enoki
(808) 533-4658
hamamur@ibm.net

Maui Aikido-Ki Society*
P. O. Box 724
Wailuku, HI 96793-0724
Attn: Shinichi Suzuki, Chris Curtis
Phone: (808) 244-5165
cdc@maui.net

Illinois

Chicago Ki Society*
926 E. Northwest Highway
Mt. Prospect, IL 60056-3444
Attn: Jonathan Eley
Phone: (847) 670-6945

Kansas

Kansas Ki Society
Attn: Andrew Tsubaki
Phone: (785) 842-3923
Dojo:
619 E 8th Street
Lawrence, KS 66044
(785) 843-8419

Midland Ki Aikido Society
9303 Johnson Drive
Shawnee Mission, KS 66222
Attn: H. Vic Montgomery
Phone: (913) 362-7314

Kansas Ki Society
International Theater Studies Center
University of Kansas
Lawrence, KS 66045
Phone: (913) 864-3534

Maryland

Montgomery County Ki-Aikido Society*
19004 Rolling Acres Way
Olney, MD 20832-1327
Dojo:
4511 Bestor Road
Rockville, MD 20853
Attn: Daniel E. Frank
Phone: (301) 871-9155

Massachusetts   Massachusetts Ki Society
184 Seapit Road
P.O. Box 457
East Falmouth, MA 02536-0457
Attn: Leonard Rose
Phone: (508) 548-7900

Minnesota   Minnesota Ki Society
4432 Ellerdale Road
Minneapolis, MN 55435
Attn: Jerry Kelly
(612) 971-6247 (day)
(612) 933-6064 (evening)
Dojo:
Minnetonka Parks and Recreation
Linberg Center
Minnetonka, MN

Missouri   **St. Louis Ki Society***
6006 Pershing Avenue
St. Louis, MO 63112
Attn: Mark Rubbert
Phone: (314) 726-5070

New Jersey   **New Jersey Ki Society***
628 Lippincott Avenue
Riverton, NJ 08077
Attn: Terry Pierce
Phone: (609) 829-7323
Dojo:
World Gym
1703 Industrial Hwy
Cinnaminson, NJ 08077

New Mexico   Albuquerque Ki Society
3015 Monta Vista
Albuquerque, NM 87106-2116
Attn: Steven G. Merley
Phone: (505) 268-0151
smerley@usa.net

Oregon

Northwest Ki Federation*
P.O. Box 2143
Lake Oswego, OR 97035-0645
Attn: Calvin Tabata, Brenda Tam, Louise Sloss
Phone: (503) 684-0185
web site: www.e-z.net/~kweek
Hutchma@teleport.com

Northwest Ki Federation Member Dojos:
Hawthorne dojo, Portland, OR
  Attn: Jon Maxson
    Phone: (503) 223-9124
Eugene dojo, Eugene, OR
  Attn: Terry Copperman
    Phone: (541) 683-5089
Corvallis dojo, Corvallis, OR
  Attn: Jake Nice
    (541) 757-2746
Salem dojo, Salem, OR
  Attn: Bob Jones
    Phone: (503) 364-9323
Southwest dojo, Tigard, OR
  Attn: Bob Hart
    Phone: (503) 684-0185

Pennsylvania

Keystone Ki Aikido
75 Aber Road
Finleyville, PA 15332
Attn: Richard A. Miller
Phone: (724) 348-6568
AikidoSue@aol.com

Philadelphia Ki Society
3101 W. Queen Lane
Philadelphia, PA 19129
Attn: Howland Abramson
Phone: (215) 732-8425

South Carolina

South Carolina Ki Society*
P.O. Box 26735
Greenville, SC 29616-1735
Dojo:
443-B Congaree Road
Greenville, SC 29616-1735
Attn: David Shaner, Eric Harrell
Phone: (864.) 234-6595

Texas

Austin Ki Aikido
211 W North Loop
Austin, TX 78756
Attn: Kathy Ferland
Phone: (512) 459-9249

Virginia

Blue Ridge Ki-Aikido
609 Market Street, #110
Charlottesville, VA 22902
Attn: Jonathan Doner
Phone: (804) 296-4254

Virginia Ki Society*
5631 Cornish Way
Alexandria, VA 22310-4018
Attn: George Simcox
Phone: (703) 971-7928
E-mail: kimas@erols.com
Dojo:
2929-E Eskeridge Road
Fairfax, VA 22031
Phone: (703) 573-8843

Washington

Evergreen Ki-Aikido
Attn: Bud Pomaika'i Cook
Phone: (425) 786-8409
Dojo:
Evergreen Learning Center
6305 Rich Road SE #B
Olympia, WA 98501
(360) 438-3788

Seattle Ki Society*
6106 Roosevelt Way, NE
Seattle, WA 98115-6613
Attn: Koichi Kashiwaya
Phone: (425) 527-2151
E-mail: aikidoki@ix.netcom.com
Kashiwaya Sensei is Chief Instructor for the Ki
Society in the United States.

Canada

Alberta

Calgary Ki Society
2836 Morley Trail N.W.
Calgary, Alberta T2M 4G7
Attn: James Angevine, Rob Cowitz
Phone: (403) 282-5323
englishd@cadvision.com

British Columbia

Vancouver Ki Society
#140 - 2268 No. 5 Road
Richmond, B.C. V6X 2T1
Phone: (604) 261-3136

Manitoba

Manitoba Ki-Aikido
Box 113
Winnipeg, Manitoba R3E 3E8
Phone: (204) 772-5705

Ontario

Aikido & Ki (Kitchener/Waterloo)
97 Victoria Street North
Kitchener, Ontario N2H 5C1
Attn: Michael E. Hogan
Phone: (519) 570-1215

Aikido & Ki (Cambridge)
36 Ainslie St. North
Cambridge, ON N1R 3J5
Attn: Michael E. Hogan
Phone: (519) 623-5300
hogansan@hotmail.com
www.angelfire.com/biz/aikidoki/aikido.html

Kingston Ki Society Aikido Club
114 Nicholson Crescent
Amherstview, Ontario K7N 1X1
Attn: Bill Bickford
Phone: (613) 384-0423
bickford@kos.net
Dojo:
Regional Correctional Staff College
Queen's University
443 Union St W.
Kingston, Ontario

Europe

For current addresses and information please contact:
European Ki Society Headquarters*
19 Rue de la Cite, 1050 Bruxelles, Belgium
Attn: Kenjiro Yoshigasaki

Finland

Suomen Ki-Aikido Yhdistys
Helsinki
Attn: Pekka Salmi
pekka.salmi@psalmi.pp.fi

Tapanilan Eran Ki-Aikido Jaos
Helsinki
Attn: Juha Kajanen
juha.kajanen@tekla.fi

Germany

Ki und Aikido Berlin*
Hedemannstrasse 11
1000 Berlin 61
Attn: Michael Winter
Phone: 030-611-69-39

Ki und Aikido Dojo Heidelberg*
Heltenstrabe 1
6909 Leiman-Heidelberg
Attn: Dagmar Kristkeitz

Ki und Aikido Heidelberg*
Heltenstr 7
6906 Leimen

Italy

Centro Ki-Aikido Torino*
V.M. Coppino 138/10 Torino
Attn: Cocco Mileto

Ki Aikido Mestre*
Via Milano, 12 Mestre
Attn: Carlo Rehata
Ki no Kenkyukai Italig*
Casella P. le 30003
Firenze 26

Ki no Kenkyu Kai Italia*
P.O. Box 3003
Firenze 26, 50100

Meishin Kan Novara*
V. le Allegra 26
28100 Novara
Attn: Gioconto Giovanni

Ronin Ki Aikido Novara*
Via Visconti 1
Cre Enel Novara
Attn: Maul Bruno, Volpe Maurizio

Firenze Centro Ki Aikido*
Via Mannelli 121/A Firenze
Attn: Mario Peloni, Gensini Carlos

Firenze Ki Dojo*
Via Gordigiani 36/C
50127 Firenze
Attn: Giuseppe Ruglioni
Phone: 39 (055)-362090
kidojo@dad.it
www.dada.it/kidojo

UK
Ki Society of the U.K.*
5 Hopkins Road
Counden, Coventry
CV 6, 1 BD
Attn: Philip Burgess

Stourberidge Ki Society*
Phisiotherapy Gymnasium
Corbett Hospital
Vicarage Road, Stourbridge
West Midlands
Attn: Glyn Simcox

Rhondda Ki Society*
Trederwen Gwaun Bedw
Cymmer Rhondda
Mid-Gran S. Wales
Attn: Robert Turner, Richard Gardiner

Netherlands
Ki en Aikido Dojo Zeeland
Dagmar van der Velde
Geldeloozepad 6
NL -4463 AJ Goes
(0031) 113-229328

Ki Society of the Netherlands
Ijsselstein Stratt 26
5121 TS Den Bosch

Sweden
Ki no Kenkyu Kai Vasteras*
P.O. Box 422
72108 Vasteras
Sweden

South America and Pacific

Brazil

Ki Sociedad de Belo Horizonte
Caixa Postal 3341
Belo Horizonte, M. G.
Basil 30112-970
Brazil
Attn: Lael Keen
Phone: 01-55-31-227-1489

Australia

Australian Ki Society*
P.O. Box 412
Byron Bay, NSW 2481
Attn: Michael Williams
Phone: 02 66 856 389
e-mail: aikido@om.com.au
Source for up-to-date information on dojos in
Australia.

Australian Ki Society Member Dojos:
Mareeba Dojo
Lot 32 Warril Drive
Kuranda, Q. 4872
Attn: Alfio La Spina

Cairns Dojo/Mossman Dojo
PO Box 413
Mossman, Q. 4873
Attn: Roby Kessler
phone: (H) 070 982 722 (M) 015 159 447

Cooran Dojo/Boreen Point Dojo
152 Pender Creek Rd. Kinkin, Q. 4571
Attn: Cate Coupe
Phone: 075 485 4482 075 485 3028

Caboolture Dojo
147 Pitt Rd. Burpengary, Q. 4505
Attn: Tony Deckers
Phone: (H) 073 888 1243
(M) 041 977 8486
spectrum@powerup.com.au

Springhill Dojo
82 Tristania Way, Mt. Gravatt East Brisbane, Q.
4122
Attn: John Hurley
Phone: 07 3343 8846

Cleveland Dojo
135 Boundary Rd.
Thornlands, Q. 4164
Attn: Thom Hansen
Phone: (H) 07 3206 1772
(M) 041 902 3700
thansen@tpgi.com.au

City Hall Dojo
GPO Box 1852 Brisbane, Q. 4001
Attn: Michael Conroy
Phone: (H) 07 3358 4322
(W) 07 3403 3391

Griffith University Dojo
PO Box 842 Springwood
Brisbane, Q. 4127
Attn: Michael Stoopman
Phone: (H) 07 3841 4848
(W) 07 3406 4113
(M) 041 878 2259
MStoopma@qmcsbne2.telstra.com.au

Uki Dojo
Lot 28 Bonnydoon Rd. Uki, NSW 2484
Attn: Steve Phillips
Phone: (H) 02 66 795 091
(M) 015 586 583
phillips@norex.com.au

New Zealand

New Zealand Ki Society*
P.O. Box 1140
Auckland
New Zealand
Attn: Mike Standford
Dojo:
North Shore YMCA Akoranga Drive
Takapuna
New Zealand
Phone: 480-7099

Singapore

Singapore Ki Society*
53 Paterson Road
Singapore 0923
Attn: Francis Chong Hong Siong
Phone: 65-467-6045

Philippines

Cebu Ki Society
KiAikido
7 F. Ramos Street, Cebu City
Philippines 60000
Attn: Max Tian, Romy Kho
Phone: 253-5590 or 255-0058
FAX: 255-0047
E-mail: romy@mozart.clynx.gsilink.com

Ki Society of the Philippines
Steps Dance Studio
Estrella St.
Bel-Air,Makati, Metro
Manila, Philippines
Attn: Mr. Chel Diokno
(632) 6317563
Attn: Mr. Ernesto Talag Sensei
(632) 7118431

UP Ki Aikido Society,
Vanguard Bldg, DMST Complex, University of
the Philippines
Diliman Campus,
Quezon City, Philippines
Attn: Mr Tom Edison V. Pena
(632) 253-4648
e-mail: tomvp@chk.upd.edu.ph

Appendix B.
Additional Exercises

Appendix B. Additional Exercises

The Three-Minute Ki Exercise for Health

Class often begins with the Three-Minute Exercise For Health. It is intended to warm and loosen the muscles and to practice mind-body coordination. You should be able to pass a *ki* test done at any point during any of the exercises.

All exercises emphasize a gentle stretch rather than force or compression. For instance, in tilting the head forward and back, think of stretching the front of the neck — and place your mind there — rather than concentrating on forcing the back of your head into your shoulders.

For details, see Tohei (1983) starting on page 120.

The Three-Minute Ki Exercise for Health

Torso

1. Torso turning
2. Side bends
3. Bending backward and forward
4. Shoulder blade stretch

Neck

5. Tilting head from side to side
6. Tilting head forward and back
7. Looking from side to side

Legs

8. Knee bends and heel raises
9. Knee stretches

Shoulders

10. Dropping one arm (*udemawashi undo*)
11. Dropping both arms forward and reverse
12. Dropping both arms forward and reverse with One-Point.
13. Wrist shaking (*tekubi-shindo undo*).

1. Torso Turning

Turning the trunk, arms swinging from side to side.

1	2	3	4	5	6	7	8
L	L	R	R	L	L	R	R

a) Rotate One-Point, turning trunk and arms.

b) Arms rise to eye level at the mid-point of movement (top view). Chest turns 90 degrees side to side, arms wrapping around chest (side view).

c) Head stays with chest.

d) Chest moves and arms follow.

e) Only arms move (body remains still) on the second count.

f) No bend at the waist.

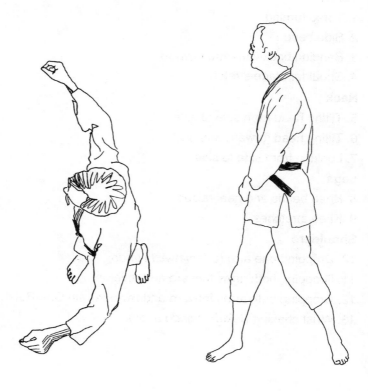

2. Bending Side to Side

This appears to be the old familiar side bend exercise from gym class but it isn't. It is, in part, a shoulder exercise.

1	2	3	4	5	6	7	8
L	L	R	R	L	L	R	R

a) On the first movement, bend to the side allowing the arm to stretch up and over the head, palm down.

b) On the second movement, trunk remains where it is. Upper arm bends at elbow. Lower arm hangs relaxed at the side.

c) Head and neck stay aligned with trunk.

3. Bending Forward and Backward

1	2	3	4	5	6	7	8
F	F	B	B	F	F	B	B

a) On the forward movement (F), *throw* the hands through the legs as though whooshing a football to someone behind you. Continue the arm swing through the legs, completely, as far as they will go but do not compress the chest by bringing the arms close together.

b) On the backward motion (B), bend back, arms following. Arms extend straight overhead and continue backward like an H, not coming together in a ^. Palms are open.

c) Eyes are straight ahead relative to head.

4. Shoulder-Blade Exercise.

1	2	3	4	5	6	7	8
L	L	R	R	L	L	R	R

a) Like 1 (Torso Turning) but elbows are bent, at shoulder height, and in a line with the plane of the back. Head and back turn together to about 130 degrees.

b) Body moves arms during the initial movement; the rear-most arm moves on second count only.

5. Tilting Head From Side-to-Side

A lateral neck exercise done by tilting the head from side to side.

1	2	3	4	5	6	7	8
L	L	R	R	L	L	R	R

a)   Hands are on hips.

b)   Bend neck, rather than raising the shoulder to meet head.

c)   Think of *stretching* and loosening the stretching side rather than *compressing* the other side.

d)   Head need not return to center; just stretch-release.

e)   Eyes and head remain forward and do not twist off axis.

6. Head Tilting Front to Back

A stretch for the front and back of the neck.

1	2	3	4	5	6	7	8
F	F	B	B	F	F	B	B

a) Hands are on hips.

b) Rather than pushing the chin into the chest (compression), think of stretching the back of the neck. To check yourself say "ahhhh" throughout. Choking or strangling noises are a sure sign of compression.

This exercise seems to cause the most problems during *ki* testing usually because of tilting the head past the center plane of the body. It is done by rotating the head, by tilting the chin up, not by rotating the base of the neck.

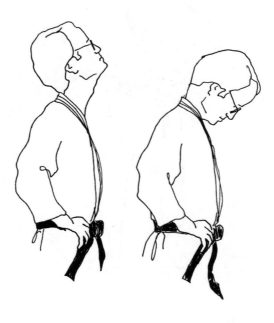

7. Looking From Side To Side

A neck exercise, turning the head from left to right.

1	2	3	4	5	6	7	8
L	L	R	R	L	L	R	R

a) Hands are on hips.

b) Look over alternate shoulders without twisting the trunk or raising the shoulders (and keeping the head vertical),.

c) Head always returns to center position.

Do the exercise while walking. If you do not return head (and eyes) to center you will become badly disoriented. Partners doing this exercise on count should only see the front of the partner's face — not the side.

8. Knee Bends And Heel Raises

These are small, rhythmic knee bends that concentrate on dropping One-Point while helping you to find the balls of your feet.

1	2		3	4	5	6		7	8
D	D	UP	D	D	D	D	UP	D	D

a) Hands on hips, feet a bit more than shoulder-width apart.

b) The pattern is down-down-UP-down-down, but emphasize the *down* (dropping weight underside), not the up; the *up* is only a means of getting to the next *down*.

9. Knee Stretches

This is an exercise to loosen and stretch the knees and hamstrings.

1	2	3	4	5	6	7	8
L	L	R	R	L	L	R	R

a)   Extend leg with toe flexed.

b)   Press down gently on the knee.

   The motion is *down* with the leg, not *in* against the knee.

c)   Think not of pushing down the knee but of *stretching* the back of the leg.

10. Arm-Dropping

With this exercise (*Udemawashi-Undo*) the rhythm changes to a single motion per count. This is not an exercise in *rotating* the arm around the shoulder. It is arm *dropping*.

1	2	3	4	5	6	7	8
L	L	L	L	R	R	R	R

a)   Raise left arm as high over the head as possible without straightening elbow.

b)   Drop the left arm (and return) four times.

c)   Drop the right arm (and return) four times.

11. *Dropping Both Arms*

This is the two-armed version of the Arm-Dropping Exercise (*Udemawashi Undo*) done forward and in reverse..

1	2	3	4	5	6	7	8
F	F	B	B	F	F	B	B

The tendency is to raise One-Point while raising the arms; the challenge is to leave One-Point in place while simply returning the arms to their starting position. Looking up through fingers you should see fingers and ceiling — not walls or thumbs. A sword is held overhead in this same position. When arms are lower, they restrict the view of the surroundings. Arms held correctly do not.

12. Dropping Both Arms While Dropping One-Point

This is the two-armed version of the Arm-Dropping Exercise (*Udemawashi-Undo*) dropping weight and One-Point.

1	2	3	4	5	6	7	8
F	F	B	B	F	F	B	B

a)   Raise both arms straight up.

b)   Drop both arms while dropping One-Point.

c)   As arms ascend, return to starting position.

13. Wrist-Shaking Exercise

As Arm-Dropping exercise ends (with arm up), continue the motion by dropping arm and blending the downward motion into vigorous shaking of the wrists (*tekubi-shindo undo*).

1	2	3	4	5	6	7	8
half	*half*	*half*	*half*	*half*	*half*	*half*	*half*

    a) Decrease the physical movement by half with each count but continue the motion internally.

    b) As physical movement decreases, visualize the molecules vibrating and moving.

Order Form

Also from Round Earth Publishing . . .

Books

Aikido with Ki — A Sampler of Aikido Exercises (available Fall 1998)
Ki in Aikido — A Sampler of Ki Exercises $16.95

Videos

The Hidden Fortress (Kurosawa) The inspiration for *Star Wars*.	*$39.95*
Samurai Trilogy (Inagaki) Musashi Miyamoto (Boxed set).	*$69.96*
Sanjuro (Kurosawa) A rollicking samurai spoof.	*$29.95*
Seven Samurai (Kurosawa) The award-winning classic.	*$34.95*
Yojimbo (Kurosawa) Inspired the Western *Fistful of Dollars*	*$29.95*

Patterns

Hakama — for Aikido, sewing/wearing/folding instructions.	*$14.95*
Hapi, Haori, Tabi — Japanese jackets and slipper socks.	*$16.95*
Kimono — Yukata style for men and women.	*$16.95*

Name (Please Print):		
Address:		
City:	State/ZIP:	
Phone: ( )	Dojo:	
Total Merchandise:	$	
Virginia residents please add 4.5% State tax:	$	
Shipping: $4.00 for up to 2 items. $2.00 each additional 2 items.	$	
Total:	$	

Credit Cards: Expiration Date:____/____

☐ VISA ☐ MasterCard   ☐ Discover ☐ AmExpress

Name on Card (PRINT):

Card Number:

☐☐☐☐–☐☐☐☐–☐☐☐☐–☐☐☐☐

Signature:

FAX your order **TOLL FREE** to 1-(888)-542-4543
71021.744@CompuServe.com   Voice: (703) 641-9169
Round Earth Publishing, P. O. Box 3855, Merrifield, VA 22116

Order Form

Also from Round Earth Publishing . . .

Books

Aikido with Ki — A Sampler of Aikido Exercises (available Fall 1998)
Ki in Aikido — A Sampler of Ki Exercises $16.95

Videos

The Hidden Fortress (Kurosawa) The inspiration for *Star Wars*.	*$39.95*
Samurai Trilogy (Inagaki) Musashi Miyamoto (Boxed set).	*$69.96*
Sanjuro (Kurosawa) A rollicking samurai spoof.	*$29.95*
Seven Samurai (Kurosawa) The award-winning classic.	*$34.95*
Yojimbo (Kurosawa) Inspired the Western *Fistful of Dollars*	*$29.95*

Patterns

Hakama — for Aikido, sewing/wearing/folding instructions.	*$14.95*
Hapi, Haori, Tabi — Japanese jackets and slipper socks.	*$16.95*
Kimono — Yukata style for men and women.	*$16.95*

Name (Please Print):		
Address:		
City:	State/ZIP:	
Phone: ( )	Dojo:	
Total Merchandise:	$	
Virginia residents please add 4.5% State tax:	$	
Shipping: $4.00 for up to 2 items. $2.00 each additional 2 items.	$	
Total:	$	

Credit Cards: Expiration Date:____/____

☐ VISA ☐ MasterCard   ☐ Discover ☐ AmExpress

Name on Card (PRINT):

Card Number:

☐☐☐☐–☐☐☐☐–☐☐☐☐–☐☐☐☐

Signature:

FAX your order **TOLL FREE** to 1-(888)-542-4543
71021.744@CompuServe.com   Voice: (703) 641-9169
Round Earth Publishing, P. O. Box 3855, Merrifield, VA 22116